*People think that grief
slowly gets smaller with time.
In reality, grief stays the same
but slowly life begins to
grow bigger around it.*

— Lois Tonkin

ALWAYS
Lessons in Loss, Love and Resilience
NOVEMBER

a father's memoir

by Arik Housley
with Holly Lynn Payne

SKYWRITER

This work depicts actual events in the life
of the author as truthfully as recollection permits.

Text copyright © 2025 by Arik Housley
Cover copyright © 2025 by Skywriter Books

Skywriter Books supports the right to free expression and the value of copyright. The purpose of copyright is to encourage writers and artists to produce the creative works that enrich our culture.

The scanning, uploading, and distribution of this book without permission is a theft of the author's intellectual property. If you would like permission to use material from the book (other than for review purposes), please contact arik@arikhousley.com. Thank you for your support of the author's rights.

Skywriter Books • 333 Caledonia Street • Sausalito, California 94965

Mailing Address: PO Box 2630 • Sausalito, CA 94966

Originally published in e-book and paperback by
Skywriter Books in November 2025
Skywriter Books name and logo are trademarks of Skywriter Books Corp.

The publisher is not responsible for websites (or their content) that are not owned by the publisher.

PERMISSIONS

Thank you to the individuals mentioned in this book who have given permission to share their name and the details of their involvement in this story.

Permission granted by Skylar Gray to print the lyrics to "Calling from Heaven"
Text copyright © 2019 by Skylar Gray

Library of Congress Cataloging-in-Publication Data available upon request.

ISBNs: 978-0-9972144-1-3 (hardcover),
978-0-9822797-9-3 (e-book), 978-8-9881081-2-2 (paperback)
Printed in the United States of America

Book cover and interior design by Tom Joyce, Creativewerks
Cover photo by Sarah Lane

for Alaina

Part One

THE UNTHINKABLE

The Call

HAVE YOU EVER had the phone ring in the middle of the night?

It's usually not a call you want to receive. My wife and I got that call.

Shortly after midnight, Wednesday, November 8, 2018, my wife's phone rang. Startled, she rolled over in bed and picked it up, not expecting to hear from our college friends Chris and Amy, who lived on Pepperdine University campus. We had all met when we were undergraduates and had been friends ever since, but talking after midnight was not a tradition we continued after college. Let's face it. It was an odd time to call.

My wife clutched the phone. Apparently, our daughter had shared dinner with Chris and Amy that night, something she did weekly since she arrived on campus. Overlooking the Pacific Ocean, Pepperdine had been our dream school, and Alaina had chosen it too. Even though we lived seven hours north in Napa Valley, Chris and Amy's proximity to

Alaina comforted us after we dropped her off in late August to begin her life as a college student. The last time we saw her was at parents' weekend in October, known as Waves Weekend. We always missed her, of course, and she missed us, but she was making friends, doing well with classes, and learning how to balance her studies and life—something we valued and wanted to instill in her. Everything was going well, until that November night.

Hannah's mouth dropped open when Chris delivered the news, and everything sounded like it was underwater. "We just wanted to let you know there has been a shooting at Borderline. A bunch of Pepperdine students were there, including Alaina."

A shooting? At Borderline? Inconceivable. We all knew what it was. A popular bar off campus in Thousand Oaks, just a few miles northwest of campus.

There was a pause that seemed to last forever before Chris spoke again. He and Amy had hosted Alaina and ten other students that night for dinner. They knew her plans so there was no way that Hannah and I could question if she was there. We knew because she had also asked us if she should go that night. We told her, yes, of course, have fun. It was our role as her parents to encourage her to experience the world. She had finished studying and was free to have fun that evening. Borderline permitted anyone eighteen and older on the dance floor every Wednesday on College Country Night to enjoy the tradition of line dancing there.

By now, Hannah had turned the phone on speaker and my stomach dropped, waiting for Chris to continue.

Part One | THE UNTHINKABLE | *11*

"We are still getting information because there are still a lot of people unaccounted for. We are waiting to hear more news."

I sat there in a daze, grasping for clarity, making up all kinds of scenarios that would keep our daughter alive. First thought: She dropped her phone when they were all escaping. Next thought: She was maybe hiding in the bar. Maybe she got out. Maybe she was trying to remember our numbers because we had been on speed dial her entire life and would not know the numbers to call if she had someone else's phone.

I reached over to my nightstand and grabbed my phone to begin texting Alaina. "I love you, Laina. Please let us know you're okay," but then I stopped. If she was still alive and people were still hiding in the building, I didn't want to be the reason he found her. I would not be able to live with myself if I had made her phone buzz and then he shot her.

I dropped my phone. Hannah hung up with Chris and looked over at me.

The only notions running through our heads in that blur of the unthinkable were hope, faith, belief, trust. It was our instinct as a couple to refuse to believe the worst.

Still, our minds reeled. Should we get in the car and start driving to Pepperdine? It was the middle of the night. We were in shock and in no shape to drive seven hours in the dark. We also did not know if Alaina dropped her phone. What if she was still in the building? What if her phone went off and the shooter was still there? We didn't know what to do.

Hannah wanted to call our dear friends, known to our children as Auntie Lorrie and Uncle Dave. At first, I was a bit hurt, thinking, *Why can't I be who you turn to right now?* Her mind was reeling as fast as mine, but Hannah was right. Dave and Lorrie would offer comfort and companionship, as they always did. We had traveled together for years and called ourselves the Hilsleys, combining both our last names. They were like family.

Hannah called Lorrie, whose daughters, Anie and Kate, loved Alaina, and had us eating at each other's homes for years when they were younger. I had known Dave since elementary school in Yountville and by then we'd spent mountains of time together. While we were outnumbered by the ladies, we always talked about work and enjoyed a drink.

Lorrie answered the phone with a groggy "Hello."

Hannah put her on speaker. "There's been a shooting at a bar where Alaina was tonight."

Lorrie snapped to. "What? Oh my God! Is she okay?"

Hannah glanced at me. "We don't know. Can you come over here?"

Within minutes, Lorrie and Dave showed up at our house while we tried to process our feelings and thoughts. Dave and I sat on the couch in the living room going through every possible scenario of hope, trying to rationalize where Alaina might be. The entire time I was trying to fight back the instinct to vomit.

Hannah and I had encouraged Alaina to go out that night. She was a nerd—she loved to read, sing, and play multiple musical instruments. She loved to be with her friends and especially eat dark chocolate. Alaina loved steak, truffle cheese, charcuterie, and coffee bean ice blended mocha, dark chocolate, of course. We wanted her to experience all of life, and she was finally having things go well for her at Pepperdine after a few initial bumps.

While she was close with a great group of suitemates and had made some other very good friends, she didn't get a bid to the sorority she wanted or make it into the choir, which was a disappointment for her because she loved to sing. However, things started to get better in late October when she made the mock trial team and was accepted into Pepperdine's International Program in Florence, Italy, for her sophomore year. Things were looking up and she was enjoying school, but she wasn't going off campus to enjoy other activities. After she finished her Great Books essay that night, we encouraged her to join her friends at Borderline and dance.

And now, we waited, and waited, never planning for the unthinkable, but facing it head on. There was no news. Waiting around seven hours north in Napa County wasn't putting us in any better position to make sense of the situation or help our daughter.

We needed to get to Pepperdine. My brother Adam lived in Los Angeles and had been in the news business for a decade. I had called him not long after our initial call with Chris and Amy, and he immediately got in his car and headed north to Thousand Oaks. He had enough experience in the media to ask questions and maybe, just maybe, he would arrive thirty minutes later and find her amidst the survivors, afraid and phoneless. We were so grateful that he could drive there and get a better grasp of the situation.

After we hung up, we stayed glued to the TV to see if we could get any more news, but by 1:15 a.m. Hannah could not watch anymore. I was scouring the screen for familiar faces. At one point I paused the screen to see if Alaina was in the huddled masses of survivors in the parking lot. The shooting had occurred around 11:25 p.m. on the 7th, so by then it was nearly two hours later and we had still not received any call or text. When we didn't see her in the parking lot, we prayed Alaina had dropped her phone in the bar and was still hiding there, or even at the hospital getting help.

We waited. And waited. To this day those early hours seem like a lifetime, bloated in hope, in the fantasy of how any parent would want this story to go.

Not my child. Not us. Not now.

We sat by our phone waiting for Alaina to call us. It felt interminable when neither of us had heard from her. The seconds were building a wall of horror around us.

We did not use the app on our phones to track our children because we trusted them and wanted to help them build a sense of responsibility, so it was not instinctual to look to find my iPhone. We never in a million years would have believed that one use case would involve identifying your child in a mass shooting.

Hannah blurted, "Wait, I have her iPhone attached to mine!" She reached for her iPhone and tapped the little icon. It popped up showing Alaina's Apple Watch was still in the building at Borderline. We had purchased it for Alaina's eighteenth birthday only four months prior. I wanted to believe that maybe it fell off during the chaos of escaping.

    Hannah looked up at me. Nauseous, I sat there with Dave and Lorrie not knowing what to say or do. We were all counting the seconds and holding our breaths. The seconds felt like minutes and the minutes like eternity.

    Nobody wanted to say what we already knew the moment we got the call from Chris and Amy. Deep down, we knew. I don't know how, but we felt it.

    We began calling our immediate family—my parents, Hannah's parents, and sisters, to let them know the possibility of such painful news. Meanwhile, my older brother, Adam, was almost at Thousand Oaks. On his way, he called to say he had been on the phone with a friend who was already on the scene. They were working on getting information and contacting the local hospitals to see if anyone had been admitted with injuries from their escape from the building. We all had hope. I hoped my parental gut instinct was wrong.

    I called Pepperdine University's main line and spoke to the operator, "My name is Arik Housley. My daughter Alaina was at Borderline tonight. Who do I speak with that can give me any information?" When I was finally connected with someone who was informed, I asked, "It was College Night, how many other students are still missing?"

    We knew Alaina wouldn't have been hovering over a drink, but rather with her friends doing her best line dancing. I hoped to learn that there were more students still unaccounted for in order not to feel so alone when I had asked how many other students were still missing. Maybe, just maybe, that meant a group of them were still making their way back to campus amidst the chaos.

The reply was stark. "Just Alaina." What I don't understand or could never have imagined was my reaction. If you told me this scenario, I would have thought I would be angry, furious even. Yet, there was a sense of relief. How could I have felt relief in that moment?

My stomach sank. I was flooded with a mix of emotions, both relief for the families of others that their loved one wasn't missing, lost, or worse, and the gut-wrenching realization that the truth had been confirmed. Alaina was still missing.

Around 2:00 a.m. Hannah and I were at different places. She wanted to book flights to LA immediately, but I felt we should wait by the phone in case they were trying to get a hold of us. *What should we do? What if they call when we are traveling and they can't reach us?* I couldn't figure out which was best.

I called my friend, Alf, to get his thoughts. He was a police officer and said he would reach out to law enforcement in Thousand Oaks. Then he put us in touch with our local chaplain, Lee Shaw. When I asked Lee what we should do, he said, "Arik, if she is alive, don't you want to be there to give her a huge hug and love her and be there for her through this moment? And if what we believe to be true—that she is no longer alive—you know you need to be there."

We booked the earliest flight we could get to Burbank, the airport closest to Thousand Oaks. Around 6:00 a.m. Hannah and I made our way to our son Alex's room. He had been sleeping the entire night, even when Dave and Lorrie had shown up. We didn't feel it was right to wake him when we did not have any more news. He was only fourteen years old. While we weren't going to delay the inevitable, we also believed it wouldn't help our son to know any earlier either. We walked slowly to his bed and tapped his shoulder.

"Hey bud, there has been an accident. We need to go down to Pepperdine for Alaina. Let's get some stuff so we can go."

He looked up from his bed and said, "Is Laina okay?"

I met his eyes and said, "We don't know, but we don't believe so."

We would leave Napa a few minutes later and return as a different family.

Being Informed

ALL I HEARD was *she is no longer alive.*

Nobody had told us this exactly, but we already knew.

The words played over and over the following hours during the blur of our travel to Burbank and the muted drive to Thousand Oaks, dubbed "One of the safest cities in America."

Every moment that ticked by was another confirmation of Alaina's death. We manically checked our phones every second, it seemed, hoping to hear something.

Anything but crickets.

Dave drove us to the airport to fly to Burbank. Everything was a blur. We were in the air and suddenly on the ground. When we got off the plane at Bob Hope Memorial in Burbank, we walked inside the terminal and were met immediately by the airport's chief of police. He rushed us outside to the curb where my brother Adam was waiting for us.

We got in the car with Adam, who shouldn't have been driving at the time due to his emotional state. While we didn't know any details then, he had all the information, which he shared with me years later. He would tell me he was in the car less than two minutes after I called him. His wife, Tamera, stayed home with their kids because they had just arrived from a trip to Northern California. It was 1 a.m. when Adam began the drive to Thousand Oaks. The highways were empty, and he made calls along the way to see what he could learn. Adam had been working with FOX Media for years and knew some of the FBI agents when he arrived at the scene; however, they also were still getting information. Adam would not learn the news officially until two hours before we did. But there he was, at the airport, having known when he met us at the curb; however, the authorities told him he must allow them to tell us. He was permitted to tell his wife, but he said nothing on that seemingly eternal drive to Thousand Oaks.

Adam had always been a great driver, but this was one of the few times in my life I was super uncomfortable with him behind the wheel. Even without him saying a word, I sensed he knew because it was highly likely that his colleagues had more information, but he abided by the protocols even though our hearts and guts had already overridden them. As we weaved around cars, honking and lunging to get through traffic, we finally made it to Thousand Oaks Teen Center. We parked a few rows away from the building because the lots were already full. As we walked toward the front door, we suddenly noticed TV cameras heading in our direction. My stomach sank. Adam looked the other way. He was a well-recognized person working in the media, and the irony wasn't lost on us when cameras were turned on his own family. We managed to get through the front doors and into the lobby without making any statements.

As we walked through the lobby of the teen center, we were greeted with tearful hugs from Chris, Amy, and our good friend Dave Roach, who had joined us for Waves Weekend only a month prior. Alaina loved Dave and enjoyed introducing us as her two dads. To say the emotions walloped us was an understatement. Amy rushed to Hannah and gave her a big hug. She choked back tears and cried out, "I am so sorry I couldn't protect her. I was supposed to protect her."

Hannah told her, "No, she is with Him now. She's okay. This was not your fault."

Amy looked at her startled. Hannah nodded and stood staring at her, resolute.

"She is with Him now," she repeated, reassuring Amy. "It is not your fault."

How Hannah could stand unfettered in her faith during the hardest moment as a mother—the day she lost her only daughter—will remain a mystery. There she was, trying to comfort her dear friend who felt somehow responsible for the events that night. Hannah knew it was not Amy's or anyone else's responsibility. Our daughter was a young adult capable of making decisions on her own, and Hannah would never have blamed anyone, or herself, for what happened that night. Our family was not wired to blame. We were built to accept.

Still, Amy was speechless as something overcame my wife. She held her ground. She stood rooted in her convictions and buoyed by her faith. It is a moment that still astounds me when I look back at how she faced this epic loss head on. Hannah would have enough faith to carry us through the emotional tsunami that would chase all of us for months.

That said, long, tearful embraces commenced with each of us.

We stood in the lobby for an hour-like minute, while the officials were told we had arrived. The next thing we knew, we were walking through a small gym with groups of people sitting huddled together. Everyone was crying. I just remember walking through and looking at faces thinking, *Is this a nightmare? When will I wake up? How is this all happening? Were they already informed? Are we skipping the line? Let them go first, they were here already.*

We weaved through the gym and out the back door of the building. By then, I was wondering where the hell we were going. I just wanted them to tell us the truth, but we were told to wait outside. I wondered if maybe they were still unsure if Alaina was one of the deceased before they told us officially. I was holding on to every strand of hope.

Someone appeared from the building next door and introduced himself. I don't remember who it was, but we followed him into the smaller building and were seated in another room. Dave, Chris, and Amy waited outside, while Hannah, Alex, and I sat in silence. Adam stood behind us, waiting for the words. Finally, a few people in uniform and some in plain clothes entered the room. They told us they were waiting for one more person to get out of another room. He finally entered and closed the door.

To be honest, I don't remember much that was said in that room. The words were blurred but confirmed what we knew in our hearts from the moment we got the call. Alaina had been killed in the shooting.

The second thing I remember was a dark-haired woman sitting across the table. Andrea immediately became a resource for us and, later, a wonderful friend. She would be our victim's advocate. She introduced herself and explained her role. "There will be a lot of things to figure out, sign, and know, but I will do everything for you. If you sign this document, it will allow me to represent you as your advocate." Hannah and I looked at each other, then we looked at my brother. He nodded, said something that I can't recall, and we signed.

Andrea was such a gift to us. She was kind and always listened. Every time another report or article was published about the shooting, she was our first line of defense. She understood that we didn't want to know the details, which would only keep us in a trauma loop that would be detrimental to our mental health and our son. We were wise to make that decision. Andrea was available to give us any details or answer questions but agreed not to say anything until we asked. She reached out to Adam only a few times to clarify a few details.

The entire experience in that room was something I will never forget. While the events and details were fuzzy, the kindness and compassion were something Hannah and I would remember forever. One bit of advice about grieving from the chaplain would become our MO. "Don't worry about dinner, tomorrow, or next week," He gently consoled us. "Try to live each moment. If you're hungry, eat. If you're tired, sleep. If you want to go for a walk, do it and if you want to cry, cry. Take the time you need and try not to worry about everything else right now."

I now tell that to anyone I meet who is facing significant loss.

It was great advice, but the emotions still come in waves—even now, five years after that dreadful time in my life. After being informed, we asked Dave, Chris, and Amy to join us while we processed our new reality. Our daughter was dead and never coming back.

And then something unexpected happened. Rather than be sucked into the dark underworld of despair, Hannah looked straight at me and said, "I want to go to Pepperdine, to the chapel!"

We left the building and were barely in the parking lot when we were suddenly met by cameras. I couldn't believe they were in our faces and still cannot understand the lack of respect the media has when it comes to chasing the story of tragedies. It's as if their moral and ethical understanding are thrown in the street and they then run it over with a big truck.

None of us had anything to say. Our emotions were flooding our brains. Who is coherent when they are traumatized? It felt like a cheap shot and made my blood boil. This wasn't the first infraction. Earlier that morning, we learned news broke on social media that "the niece of Adam Housley and Tamera Mowry-Housley" had been shot. The posts suspiciously showed up prior to our official notification from authorities. Adam had been in television for years and Tamera is extremely well known for her role in *Sister, Sister* and many other television productions for decades. Apparently, their media status made Alaina's murder more newsworthy and worth mentioning—even before her own parents found out. I found out years later that one of Alaina's suitemates was messaged on Instagram inquiring if she had a statement in the event that Alaina's murder was official. This was unconscionable but happens all the time, unfortunately.

Thankfully, my brother was a pro at handling tragic news and refused to tell us, having been advised to let the professionals inform us. The advice was spot on. I can't imagine if he had told us before we boarded the plane to Burbank or when we got into his car. It forced us to be with our emotions—to be present in our pain. It was the best advice, and I wouldn't change a thing about how we were informed. If it had been any different, I might not have received the chaplain's compassionate advice to live in the moment. That suggestion would become our true north. But we weren't ready to go there. We needed solace. We needed something beyond our capacity to cope with our new reality. We needed hope, and Hannah would find it at the chapel.

Pepperdine

WE DROVE TO the posh beachy coastal town of Malibu and up the hill to Pepperdine's campus, with the midday sun shining across the Pacific Ocean. Everything felt still and strangely on hold until all our gut instincts had been validated. The air was charged with the kind of heat and dryness that arrived with the fires or earthquakes in California. We could not make sense of any of this then, as everything played out in slow motion. To this day, recounting it seems as if it was all just a dream, and most days I wish it had been. It's only natural to want to wake up from it, to be nudged one morning with my wife whispering in my ear, "It was only a dream." But my wife was already on another trajectory, and perhaps deep down she knew that we had already been awakened and our waking state would never change.

Hannah would lead me to where I needed to be held—embraced by a deep and unshakeable faith that no matter how awful this entire situation would be, it was our truth to accept it, and we would find our way through the pain. Together. There are times when I look at my wife and realize, again and again, how lucky I am to have met her. They say we marry the people with whom we will do the most spiritual work within our life, but we never could have imagined the work we would be called to do. That day, we began walking down a new path. Not of hate. Not of malice. Not of revenge, regret, or rage. Faith was dancing with my wife, and soon with me.

Hannah took me back to Pepperdine and to Stauffer Chapel where we once gathered as undergrads. The entire campus overlooks the Pacific Ocean, and on the clear days, boasts stunning views of the coast. No matter where you look, beauty is there. Pepperdine had brought us together, and it had called our daughter into its domain. We knew every nook and cranny of that campus and that morning, we were grateful to get a highly sought after token to get into the reserved parking lot near the Stauffer Chapel, one of the most peaceful and serene spots on campus with ocean views.

We parked and walked toward the chapel. The massive stained-glass wall behind the pulpit in all its colors and shapes radiates a beauty and spiritual nature. Even on the most overcast days with coastal fog, the light has a way of finding the stained glass and making the space feel so uplifting. Hannah approached the doorway and took in a deep breath before we were met by friends. I had intuited that Pepperdine was the place everyone would gather, yet she knew the chapel was the place for us to be at that moment. She was right and it was the best possible place we could be.

The first couple to meet us were Hung and Corrinne Le who offered tearful embraces.

Hung was on staff when Hannah and I were students at Pepperdine, and he is the reason I decided to study abroad. Twenty-five years earlier, Hung had called me into his office.

I walked in and sat down and said, "What's up, Hung?"

He said, "Arik, are you applying to study abroad?"

"I don't think so, I don't think my parents would be okay with it and it's more money."

He responded, "It costs the same as if you are on campus here, except the flights and some travel expenses. You're going! If you could choose, where would you go?"

I said, "I think Florence. I already speak pretty good Spanish and there is no Spanish-speaking program, plus who doesn't love Italian food." I left his office and asked my parents that night. Although they were hesitant at first, they supported my decision. I took the plunge and went. Living in Italy was a life changer. I adopted the work-to-live, not live-to-work mindset. Hung and Corinne still remain great friends to this day. Their unwavering faith was inspirational to so many of us. Seeing them that day was like a lifeline. So many emotions ran through us as we processed the unthinkable. The next couple of hours were a bit of a fog of tears, hugs, and music. Many faculty and students came to offer condolences. Some said nothing but offered a hug instead and others, it seemed, were asking for a hug. I thought comforting others amid our own pain was hard to get used to, yet it was natural for us. These were the first of many times where we would find ourselves consoling others who were also deep in grief. We eventually came to understand: They loved Alaina and were deeply hurt too.

At one moment, I took in a breath to ground myself and looked up at the stained-glass window in the chapel. I was overcome by feelings of beauty and pain all at once seeing others affected by this tragedy who could not look at us. It was startling at first. Nobody had warned us that some people who were so paralyzed by fear would pretend not to see us or avoid eye contact. It's as if they could not bear our grief and, for some reason, held shame for not being able to do so. I stood there, unconsciously trying to reconcile this as people came into the chapel to find us.

An acoustic guitarist played for a while as students and faculty came and went into the chapel. The news had spread everywhere by now. Some people would pray, some just wanted to give their condolences, and soon many dear friends arrived. At one point, I remember Dave Roach taking Alex out to get some air. Alex was only fourteen years old but already exhibiting grace in the way he was handling this news. His strength and resilience through the entire process were exemplary, and I was stunned at how he seemed more capable than me in dealing with his sister's murder.

Everyone who gathered in the chapel that day was traumatized but offered their presence and support. It was a wonderful gift for Dave to take Alex out for a bit, and we had to trust that he would be okay. It was not our instinct to clutch on to him; he needed to find his own way of processing this too and Dave's instincts to lead him away from us, for a short break, would help establish his own ability to metabolize grief. Rather than grip him and project our fear of losing him, too, we wanted him to feel safe. We learned that grasping is an instinct for many parents who have lost a child, but it can be extremely unfair to the surviving siblings and does not support their healing. Seeing Alex leave us for a short moment made us all stronger in taking our next steps together.

After he returned, we made our way to the Center for Communications and Business, which required the dreadful 150-stair climb up the Malibu hillside to the building that houses the university TV and radio station and other classrooms. "ComPad" was what we called it in the mid-1990s, when it was one building and some portables. Now it is a state-of-the-art facility. Rather than climb the stairs, we were told we could park in front—a small consolation given the chain of events. We were taken to a room with food for everyone and for the next few hours, greeted a hundred more people who came to show their support, including my current *Sigma Chi* fraternity brothers, twenty years younger than me and whom I had never met. Some brothers stayed to chat with Alex, yet most of them just offered their presence, which was appreciated. Sometimes just being with us was the best thing anybody could have done to support us. One's presence is truly the best present. It is so undervalued most times, but really, it's what matters most and makes the biggest difference in how you recover from any kind of loss—large or small. I loved the maturity of these young fraternity brothers and felt comforted by them. I know Alex felt the same.

Friends from all over Southern California were driving up the coast to be with us. Included in this motley crew of angels was the VP of Student Affairs, Connie Horton, whose team reached out to let us know they were putting us up near campus in a home owned by Pepperdine where we were invited to stay as long as we needed. Then another woman reached out to see what we would like stocked in the fridge. I stared at her, perplexed. Food hadn't crossed my mind. It would be one of many instances where the trauma had shut me down, as it does to anyone.

"I have no idea," I told her. "Water and bananas, maybe?" Are we leaving to go home tomorrow morning? If so, we barely need anything. If not, would we stay for a few days to work with the coroner or law enforcement? Answering a question about food stumped me. I couldn't answer. My mind couldn't think outside of that moment.

The woman explained she would fill the fridge with breakfast foods and snacks in the event friends would visit, but she told me she couldn't get alcohol because of the school's policies. "I totally understand, thank you," I said.

Everything was moving slow and fast, but I so appreciated the university's gesture in helping us and making decisions on our behalf. This was a learning moment that I would use for others. It's okay to make the decisions for others in deep distress, when the pain is too much to bear and the mind cannot think clearly.

Now, I tell others to keep it simple. Don't ask the bereaved anything too logical. The simple gesture of filling a fridge with breakfast foods and snacks is a huge gift on its own. At the same time, don't take it personally if they don't eat or drink what you brought. I would soon learn that the smallest gesture would have the biggest impact, when the moment was right for it. While I don't remember the woman's name, her gesture was perfect, and it taught me a wonderful gift I suggest to others: Don't ask. Just do it, gently, with no expectation of any response. Just do it in kindness.

Shortly after that, Alaina's godparents, Jake and Kassy Flesher, called to tell us that they were on their way from Sacramento. They had initially heard the news of the shooting and continued to prepare for their day when they got word Alaina was at the bar and likely one of the victims. They were the ones who came the farthest to be with us. Jake and Kassy are dear friends we met at Pepperdine. While they both ended up transferring, we always kept in touch and remained close friends. Even though we didn't see each other frequently, the minute we reconnected we were taken back to the same nineteen-year-old idiots we were when we met. Jake and I shared that level of comfort, and it was like no time had passed that day.

The stream of kindness continued.

When Connie Horton's team arrived to supply the house, they informed us that the owner of the Malibu toy store donated some Legos and puzzles so that the kids would have something to do. In the midst of the trauma, there was no way we could consider those details, but we really appreciated them. Although Alex was fourteen, he had always loved Legos, so it was fun seeing him building stuff with our friends' children—which helped them all take their minds off our reality. A few weeks later, when we returned for Alaina's memorial service, I visited the toy store. I wanted to personally thank the shop owner and tell them how much it meant to us. I then bought a $50 gift card for the next person who walked in and asked them to give it to them after I left. I also left my Alaina's teal bracelet with "Kindness Matters" printed on it. I liked not knowing who received the small gift. I just wanted to pay the kindness forward.

While Connie and her team set out the nourishment, the house was filled with more than twenty-five people. There was nothing else to do but gather, eat, drink some wine (that someone made a special trip to bring to the house), and let the kids play Legos. It was all so bittersweet, this beautiful moment of love and kindness in the midst of such deep sorrow.

To this day, we don't really understand how we seemed to have skipped the stages of grief. And I'm not sure that we actually had. It was obvious we were traumatized, but there was something else going on that Hannah and I continue to marvel at and discuss to this day. We trusted the sequence of events that night. Hannah and I assumed that Alaina was in the right place at the right time when evil walked in. She had finished her schoolwork, then showed up in full force to the mock trial team (by blowing their doors off with an unexpected plan covering a whiteboard), then she went to a convocation dinner at Chris and Amy's house. She was doing exactly what she was supposed to do as a college student. She was living her life.

While we sat in the home that Pepperdine provided, surrounded by our loved ones, I could not help but wonder if it was all just a bizarre dream. So many emotions and thoughts collided and contradicted each other. It felt real and unreal. It felt calm and chaotic. Trauma trips a lot of wires.

As Thursday, November 8th, drew dark, many of our friends left to drive to their homes in Southern California, and those who were staying with us at the house started to settle in. We had no idea what time we went to bed. We were all exhausted physically, mentally, and emotionally. The air was charged with the Santa Ana winds that were howling outside around seventy miles per hour and shaking the windows in the house. These are the winds that, according to ER doctors, fill hospitals with the victims of freakish accidents and induce the worst behavior in humans. The winds did not make for peaceful sleeping under any circumstances, yet we managed to drift off after a few glasses of wine to ease the blunt edge of the news.

Around 3 a.m. I awoke and saw that Hannah wasn't in bed, so I got up and began to search the house. Tracy, Alaina's other godmother and one of Hannah's dearest friends, was on the couch, but I couldn't find Hannah with her. I felt my chest tighten when I searched the room and still did not see her. The house was huge. I made laps through the dining room, kitchen, living room, wending my way through the circular interior of the house. I searched the nook, reading room, entry, still nothing. I couldn't find her. My wife was missing.

The wind was howling so fiercely now it was almost haunting. My body shook with the glass rattling inside the window casings. I walked outside, thinking, *Holy shit, do I just look for her in the pitch black? How far could she have gone? Where do I start to look?* My gut tightened. I was afraid she'd broken down and went for a walk. I stood there, feeling my heart pound, unsure what to do. In the midst of that bone dry heat and searing wind swirling around me, I retraced my steps. Back at the house, I saw an extra set of feet sticking out of the blanket on the couch. Without shining my light in their faces and waking them up, I confirmed it was Hannah on the couch with Tracy. Relieved, I went back to bed and tried to fall back asleep.

Holy shit. Holy shit. Holy shit.

I lay in bed, feeling a strange tightness in my whole body, wondering if I was having a panic attack, which I had never had. Things were feeling odd. Off. Like it wasn't just Alaina's news that kept me from falling deeply asleep. The winds refused to die down but somehow, I managed to drift off with them screaming outside—giving voice to what all of us were feeling.

I was woken up by Jake around 5 a.m. He looked disheveled and panicked. "Arik, we need to get out of here."

I bolted out of bed. "What? Why?"

"I have been listening to the scanner for a while and the fire is coming this way."

"What fire?"

"The Woolsey Fire. We need to evacuate!" he said and pulled me out of the bed.

I remember thinking, *Fire? What's fucking next?*

The winds. They would spread flames fast and far and hurl them like baseballs from a vicious pitcher. Being natives of California, we knew we had to move fast, so we woke the sleeping people and grabbed our stuff. We said goodbyes and gave some hugs to a few who would head home. We were all on the road by 5:30 a.m. and headed back toward Santa Monica with the Santa Ana winds howling and screeching an unwelcome serenade in our hell.

Resilience & the Grief Timeline

TO THIS DAY, I don't understand the calm that Hannah and I had assumed from the minute we got the call. I don't know if we already knew, deep down, and had already accepted the horrific truth. Or if we were in such a state of trauma that we were simply surviving the horror show, second by second. I don't know where the mysterious sense of knowing came from, but it led us to make decisions and respond in ways for which we had no prior training. We were not first responders, but we were being hurled into the flames—quite literally—and had to deal.

After rushing out of Malibu on Friday morning to avoid the Woolsey Fire, we drove to Santa Monica, gathering there with Hannah's sisters, Leticia and Theresa, their parents, Tracy, Jake, Kassy and their kids at Coffee Bean and Tea Leaf off Third Street promenade. After Jake and Kassy left to drive back to Sacramento, Tracy booked some hotel rooms for us near LAX, assuming we would fly home the next day. What followed were some hours walking around town until we could get into the hotel, but the rest felt like a fog. We spent some time at Adam and Tamera's house later that day, where we had a chance to digest the news and maybe that was the beginning of processing it. I don't know. Trauma does funny things to the brain—helping us stay alive but isolating some of the horror, I think, and helping compartmentalize the pain so that daily life is possible.

Either way, there was such a calm over us that I could not fully understand. Never in my life could I have imagined the nightmare we were having, yet surrounded by so much love, we were able to handle it with grace. At the same time, emotions would come roaring back. I don't know what was happening to keep us so calm and I won't pretend to ever truly comprehend it. All I can say is that maybe God had wrapped His arms around us. We felt held.

That evening, Hannah and I came and went between hotel rooms. Her family was staying in the rooms next door and Alex was in our room, sitting on the bed, with his laptop. As I entered, he looked over and closed his laptop. I asked, "What are you doing, bud?"

He looked up from the bed. "I just finished writing my speech for Alaina's funeral."

I stared at him in disbelief. He nodded.

I leaned against the doorframe, thinking, *Holy shit. My son wrote his sister's eulogy.*

If ever an irony had struck me, this one nearly cold-cocked me with astonishment and inspiration.

Up until that moment, I had no intention of speaking publicly or privately. I was still trying to keep myself busy, as it was in the idle moments when the emotions came like a crashing wave. I could not even find the words to discuss what had happened, or why, or how I felt about it, as the emotions were colliding every second of the day and night. I didn't think I could stand up in front of anyone, much less a crowd, and speak without having a breakdown. I didn't assume Hannah would either. But our son was showing us that he had enough resilience and courage to do it. I stared at him, thinking, *I am your father, and I can do it too.*

While the Woolsey Fire raged into the hills above Malibu, devouring the canyon and driving all the residents out of Pepperdine and the surrounding area, we hunkered down in Playa Vista with some friends at Adam and Tamera's house. Life was moving us around like we were inside an old-fashioned pinball machine. Everything felt a little surreal and out of control.

Every moment I kept checking on Alex and Hannah, yet despite their moments of sorrow, they were both so composed. Please understand, composure in that moment was not emotionless, it was accepting of the emotions as they came. We continued to communicate with each other as much as possible without prying, just in case one of us was in a moment of processing the chaos.

Although I'm a pretty measured guy, I kept experiencing bits of time as if they were just slipping away. The advice from the chaplain resonated and I remembered to slow down, take in every moment and trust the process. We were functioning as best as we could. Some could call it strength, but we were simply surviving from one moment to the next, avoiding any big decisions as it was already hard enough to decide what to eat, what to wear, what to do, what to think when everything was colliding—thoughts, feelings, and memories of the last time we had seen our daughter alive. We figured it was good that we were all still showering. In the intensity that is spun from trauma, things can get strange fast—for the worst and sometimes for the best.

Life was leading my family forward. If we could learn to take things one day at a time and no faster, we could survive the acute pain. Day by day. Sometimes the grief clock is run by angels, if you allow them to show up. If you say yes to their invitations.

On day three after the shooting, I got a message from a close friend and fraternity brother who lived in the Los Angeles area. I hadn't seen my buddy Billy for a while but was happy to see his name and read his message.

"Would you like to meet my son, Tasso?"

I showed his text to Hannah. She smiled, then reached out and squeezed my hand. I felt a mix of emotions and my eyes watered. I was so happy to hear that Billy wanted to see us. Tasso was his first child, and having just lost our first child, our answer to Billy was, "Yes! We'd love to meet your son!"

Billy and I had met in the second semester of my freshman year. He was a sophomore and had returned from studying abroad in London. He moved into the dorm suite I shared with Bob. I looked up to Billy. He was smart, sometimes funny, and always empathetic. We shared a lot of laughs in our dorm. There was a lot of hazing from the local (non-national) fraternities, so Billy and his friend Levi started a fraternity with intentions to follow *Sigma Chi*. Billy and Levi had built a group of close friends with intent to do more service than the service fraternity and not to allow hazing. Many of us were in student government and somewhat inseparable, and after I returned from study abroad the next year, Billy and the guys approached me to join more than fifteen others who had already committed to be in this new fraternity. While I wasn't into the fraternity concept, I couldn't imagine anything but being with my friends. We were friends first.

Sometimes when you say yes, it comes back to hold you later in the most unexpected moments. We would laugh for hours and enjoy doing stupid stuff like playing dorm golf (one club and a tennis ball, always dressed like an idiot) or sliding down the wet grass on the front hill below the cross at the front of campus, all the while wrapped in trash bags (our own personal slip and slide; it was unsuccessful). They were precious moments, unscathed by the realities of life, and I was always happy to relive them and shoot the shit with Billy about the "good days" because just like us, Billy had already survived trauma and deep loss. It was one of the reasons he offered us the opportunity to meet his son soon after we lost Alaina. If he hadn't been through his own loss, he would not have understood how important it was to show others how to move forward on the turnpike called trauma. We could trust him.

Soon after returning from London, Billy dated a close friend of ours named Tessie. Tessie was always funny and kind. We all loved her. She would sit in a room with all of us stupid guys and allow us to walk up and practice our pick-up lines. She would let us know how bad they were and we would laugh for hours. Everyone loved her, but Billy was *in* love with her.

Shortly after college, Tessie was diagnosed with ovarian cancer. Billy and Tessie were head over heels for each other and, despite the diagnosis, got engaged and married. Hannah and I had also been engaged and planned to be married on the same day, so we moved our wedding date up a week in order for our friends to go to both weddings in August of 1998.

After their marriage, Tessie went through some cancer treatments and received some great news. The doctors thought they had gotten everything, but six months later, the cancer returned. This cycle happened over and over again, stretching their young marriage into a few years of fighting cancer. Tessie finally passed after multiple fights with cancer when we were in our mid-twenties. Billy was distraught. He had lost the love of his life. We all shared in his pain. While we were all having our first babies, Billy was now single and navigating his grief alone.

Billy was the friend I always looked up to as a leader in our fraternity and on campus. He would listen and respect others, yet he had a quiet confidence. After Tessie's passing, he struggled with his grief for nearly a decade. He was fighting his own battle, day after day, feeling the hole in his heart. People kept trying to fix him up, all with good intentions, because he's a great man and they wanted to see him happy again. But as Billy might tell you, grief has a timeline. You can't force it. Fool it. Bribe it. Or cheat it. Sometimes it consumes you, and that is okay. Sometimes it surprises you with new ways to see your loss. Only three days into our journey with grief, my wife, son, and I were already representing three distinct ways people go through this ordeal. Some say it's an initiation of the soul, and I would agree. But Billy would be the first to show us that the light returns after a long darkness, life goes on and the hole in the heart might just sprout a flower, as it did for him.

One day Billy gave in to the online dating app scene and met Diana, an amazing woman, and it didn't seem to take long for him to see how amazing she was as a human being. He asked her to marry him, and the rest is history. Billy is now happy to call Diana his wife. They had a beautiful wedding that Hannah and I were fortunate to attend. We have a great picture of Hannah in a pink dress, where she looks like a stunner, and is laughing hysterically because the best man Levi is on the mic. Levi was always the friend who would make things either uncomfortably or outrageously funny; either way we would always be laughing around him. At the same time, he is one of the sincerest individuals I have ever known. He is the "Ted Lasso" of our friends—hilarious, witty, and kind, all wrapped into one.

When Billy showed up with Tasso, an immediate energy that entered the room. Tasso at first was hesitant to engage with me. After thirty minutes in the living room of my brother's house in Playa Vista, Tasso was toddling around checking stuff out. I had been bribing him with some Yogi snacks, which seemed to get him to warm up to me.

At that moment, I looked at Billy and said, "Tasso is here because Tessie is not." We both started tearing up in agreement, disbelief and joy—all in one. Billy had struggled with grief for many years yet was blessed to meet Diana and through this marriage, Tasso was born. This would not have been possible if Tessie had lived. This little bundle of life, love, hope, and joy was with us.

This was the moment I found my faith. Not knowing the plan is a hard concept for many to accept. The only thing certain is the unknown. I could trust there would be more unexpected events to awaken my journey of grief and faith, especially if I had any hope of staying resilient.

It's Okay to Accept Help

HOW DO YOU return to your life after the unthinkable happens? How do you resume your normal routine? How do you face your friends, other family members, and community without feeling the pity and sorrow and discomfort that your trauma has introduced into your world?

These are the questions that my family faced, as well as so many others who also have survived the unthinkable. There is no hierarchy of loss. Once death takes a loved one, the why and how don't affect the survivors as much as not knowing how to cope without them.

Let me state something I say repeatedly: We all do this grief journey differently and that is okay. There is no perfect way, and my grief doesn't rank higher than your grief. Grief is grief.

We were about to return to the void. We were about to walk back into our home, knowing that our daughter would never enter it again. The finality of that would strike me on the flight back, and yet somehow, I knew we would be okay. We would find our way forward. Day by day.

One of the keys to that progression would be to do something that I found uncomfortable: Accept help. Even ask for it. But it's the best thing I've ever learned from my brother, Adam, and it would be just like Alaina to set me up for something that would stretch me beyond my comfort zone. Sure, it was easy to give. We had been that kind of family. Givers have the power. It's those who have to receive who are the most vulnerable. Vulnerability can make us feel very uncomfortable. We think there are strings attached, or that we don't deserve another's help. Or a free pass. Or whatever form the help shows up in. The point is that loss brings people together and creates the perfect conditions for learning how to give help and how to graciously receive it. Let's just say Alaina was probably setting up all kinds of scenarios to see how much we'd grow.

Even though we had already booked a return flight on Southwest, there were other opportunities in the works. While we were packing our things in the hotel room, I got a message from a dear friend, Paul. His family owned a successful business, and he offered to send their company plane down to pick us up and fly us home, instead of taking a commercial airline. My immediate response was, "No, thank you so much for the kind offer, but no." It felt ridiculous to accept that kind of help. It felt excessive. It made me feel guilty. I have no idea why.

Sitting in the family room of Adam and Tamera's laid-back beachy-country home, I looked at my loved ones and told them the message I had received. Alex sat up on the couch, eyes lit up like, *Hell yeah, we will fly home in a private jet.* He didn't have to say it; I could read his face.

I looked at Hannah. Her eyes were wide too and she took a deep breath and blinked. She wasn't saying *yes* or *no*, but I could tell she was thinking, *Why not? Alex would love it.*

I loved my son for his unfiltered response. I loved my wife for her filter. She understood my hesitation and she wasn't going to be the one deciding. She knew it didn't matter. But that wasn't the point. My brother finally spoke up as if he had just heard the entire silent conversation.

"Arik, people are going to offer some things to you because they want to."

I drew in a breath. "That is just too expensive. We will be fine."

Adam persisted. "Look, they aren't worried about how much it costs. They are very aware of this. But if they didn't want to offer, they wouldn't," he said and locked eyes with me. "It's okay to accept this from them. There will be more things people do because they want to and that's okay."

I stood there for a moment, weighing our options, considering everything we had gone through. I suddenly flashed on an overbooked commercial flight, dealing with boarding it after everything we had just endured. The cattle call of Southwest Airlines just felt like one more thing to survive.

Nobody talked while I debated some more. Our father had raised us to be self-sufficient. To figure things out on our own. We represented the American modus operandi,

"We're fine, thank you, and we can handle it ourselves." I glanced up at the ceiling, wondering if Alaina was watching me debate this, making such a big deal out of our flight home. I swear I heard her laugh. *Seriously, Dad! Take the private jet.* I finally nodded.

"Alright. I'll see if the offer still stands."

Alex looked over at his mom and smiled.

We'd take the jet. With gratitude. No guilt. Adam nudged my shoulder.

"Good call," he muttered.

Looking back, I am grateful we took the private jet. We needed a safe space to process everything we would face when we touched down in Napa. I was so relieved to have nobody else to deal with other than my wife, son, Hannah's parents, Ernie and Lettie, and the pilot. It was a generous and perfect gift to us at a time we needed it most. Paul and the private jet would be remembered forever. Paul knew to give us something before we could even ask for it.

The key was saying yes.

That is something I try to tell people, especially ones dealing with grief. Accept the help people offer. People will say many times to those dealing with loss, "If there is anything you need, please tell me." Most people truly mean it, but the sad part, it often falls on deaf ears. The receiver doesn't often know what they need so they don't know how to ask for it. And while the offer is nice, most people do not know what you would want or need either. It takes two here. My brother was right. It's okay to accept their offers. It's okay to request help. Speaking from experience, don't be afraid to accept kindness. No matter how small, kindness heals. For some it is their way of showing their love and support without having to verbally express their feelings.

Later that afternoon, we made the trek from Adam and Tamera's home to the Santa Monica Airport. The traffic was much worse than expected, even though that is normal for LA. The dark night with the blur of all the headlights and the lack of sleep made me tired. We finally got to the airport and found our way to the proper area for private planes.

We were introduced to the pilots and shown the procedure. As we walked on the tarmac to board the private jet, Alex looked so excited. It was a great moment for us, seeing him smile again. We got in and sat down. This was so nice. Alex looked up and said, "We need to fly this way every time!"

Hannah replied, "Next time, we are probably back on Southwest so don't get used to it." Alex declared that when he became a professional soccer player, he would fly this way again. We all agreed that was a good plan, for now.

Landing at Napa Airport was a bit surreal. There was no security, no baggage claim, and we were ten minutes from home. I could see how Alex or anyone could get used to that form of travel. Perhaps it was Alaina's way of cushioning our landing. Because it all felt a little surreal. We had stepped off the plane into the "afterward," not knowing what life would hold for us, but Paul and so many of our friends who offered help were showing us that we would be held.

Community Support

TO OUR GREAT surprise, our afterward was anything but morose. Our community was in full force, making sure we returned to their support. I remember flowers and gifts everywhere when we got home. We had not anticipated this kind of display and figured we would maybe have a glass of wine or two then go to bed. We were mentally, physically, and emotionally drained—yet we were surrounded by this outpouring of kindness, which would continue the very next day.

Although Lorrie was also grieving and her daughters Anie and Kate were devastated, Lorrie stayed multiple nights at our house to be there for us. How she could muster the strength to leave her daughters each night after seeing us lose our daughter I have no idea. Yet during the day she would go to work as a teacher and another dear friend, Kristi would stay during the day. Our dearest friends came, gave, sat, helped and just loved. The time and care poured out to us by so many, including the layer of spouses who supported them. Then the next layer and the next. Community within community within community. We just had to remain open.

Our community—rooted in the restaurant industry—was hard at work, handling our collective grief with food. As a native of Napa Valley, there is nothing more comforting and familiar than food, and when you don't know how to plan, having food already prepared for you is one less thing to worry about. We learned this as kids, and it was about as close to growing up in Italy as we could get. Food is the language with which we learn how to gather and sometimes grieve. We have survived devastating wildfires, droughts, and unfathomable devastation. We are a community who understands how to keep going when the worst possible situation becomes our reality.

Hannah and I are partners in a restaurant, Il Posto Trattoria, with our dear friends, Justin and DeeAnn Graffigna. So it wasn't surprising they had been very busy preparing for our return. Justin and DeeAnn shared a fun bond with Alaina, always working Bottlerock—Napa's annual Memorial Day weekend music festival—in our food booth. We would always make meatball sandwiches. One year, Alaina made Justin a special sign to put on the booth with a picture of a meatball sandwich and the words: *How do you like our balls?* He howled. That was Alaina, she got her sarcasm from her father. Although the Bottlerock folks wouldn't have approved, Justin and DeeAnn loved Alaina's sense of humor. We ended up hanging the sign inside our tent and still pass the picture back and forth.

When we got up Sunday morning, we found trays of breakfast burritos from Soda Canyon Store. I wasn't sure how many folks were coming for breakfast, but this was a huge number of burritos. Many more meals followed. Lunches. Dinners. Justin had coordinated meals for nearly thirty people for weeks from Bistro Don Giovanni, Coles Chop House, Allegria, Tarla, Fume, and many others. We had so many people at the house, it was such a wonderful and kind gift from many of the owners and/or managers who have been friends for years. I can't explain how our table was covered in platters of food all day, every day. It was crazy and so kind.

One of those dinners was brought by Chef Philippe Jeanty, a very successful chef and owner of Bistro Jeanty in Yountville. My parents were his landlords. They all shared a deep mutual respect and a stubbornness. Philippe and my dad had some arguments over the years running the business, but they always appreciated one another based on their business success. As time went on and I became the intermediary, their relationship improved. They've always been friends but continued to share a respectful competitive nature.

One evening Philippe let us know he would be delivering dinner from Bistro Jeanty. He arrived at our house with a full spread. *Foie gras*, deviled eggs, and *charcuterie*. Philippe himself delivered and prepared the presentation. We enjoyed every bite.

As he was getting ready to leave, I could see the sorrow in his eyes. He is the father of two daughters and said something to the effect of, "I am so sorry. I don't know how you're doing this." I shared this same response with so many who asked the same question: "This community wrapped its arms around my family in our deepest sorrow. You'd be surprised what strength you can muster when you have an entire community behind you." From that moment, every business dealing with Philippe has been different. The empathy he showed that day and the real father I saw in my dining room changed our relationship and friendship forever. I don't know if I can ever thank him enough for his compassion and sincerity. It was as if someone was orchestrating these moments, beyond our understanding but within our capacity to receive them.

Justin continued to lead the meal coordination, rallying so many to come to our aid. We had seen firsthand how much the restaurant industry gives back after fires, earthquakes, and other unexpected events that require recovery, and we were so grateful and blessed to have such a close-knit business community. Anyone who's been lucky enough to enjoy the culinary experiences of Napa Valley can understand what a gift this was and continues to be to us.

The support extended beyond the restaurant industry. We heard there was a candlelight vigil at Vintage High School on the evening of November 8. My parents, Art and Judy, described it as a sea of people as far as they could see on the football field. We were at Pepperdine at the time, but this was one of many moments we would hear about later.

Our friends, Mark and Sarah from England, also reached out to see how they might help. We were a mess of emotion on the call when they told us they were flying over for Alaina's funeral.

At first, I protested. "Mark, thank you but it is very expensive, especially with this short notice!" He told me, "I view Alaina like a little sister. We are coming!" I remembered my brother's advice. Say *yes* to accepting things like this while navigating the grief. I was so touched. Another long-time friend, Andy, also flew over from England. Our friends found out and put the three of them up in their guest house at the James Cole Winery. It was so comforting having them with us as we shared a history of being their host family when they came as youth soccer coaches in 2007. Alaina and her friends were enrolled in their camps and Alex was jealous. He was too young, at three years old, to join, but when Andy and Mark returned to the house each day after practice, they would run around with all the kids, swimming and having fun like older siblings. To say they became friends is an understatement; they became family. Not long after Mark returned to England, he met Sarah and we grew our friendship.

We stayed close with them so when Mark and Sarah (now his wife) insisted they were coming for Alaina's funeral, I knew I could not say no. They wanted and needed to be here, not only for us, but for themselves. They loved Laina and we loved that they had made the trip.

When the world shut down during the COVID-19 pandemic, we ended up living in our home together, not long after losing Alaina. While much of the world's population felt isolated and alone, we felt surrounded by the love and community that Mark and Sarah brought to us, and we formed a makeshift family.

When I look back at all the ways people showed up for us when we least expected, I am filled with gratitude. It is one thing to have lost a family member, and another to bear witness—as a friend—to that loss while grieving. It takes so much strength and courage to show up for others like this. Like when our friends helped us choose Alaina's gravesite. That was dirty work, literally. These are the moments that define a friendship, give it roots, and allow it to hold you up for the rest of your life.

Finding My Voice

THE DAY AFTER we flew home, November 11th, the Hero Foundation organized a March Against Gun Violence at Napa's Memorial Stadium. Hannah and I had no idea if we would go. We were still processing everything and living in that liminal space between overwhelm and emotional flooding. We wanted to show up for everything our community was doing on Alaina's behalf and had found out that morning about the march from her friends and others who were going. At the time, we did not know much about the Hero Foundation, only that it consisted of young adults in Napa County who respond to the needs of the community and believe the world needs heroes.

While that would have been enough to say yes, we had some reservations. While we certainly could have used a hero that day and many since, we considered a lot of unknowns while we drank coffee and ate another breakfast burrito. Hannah and I were unsure we should go to the march. It would be our first public appearance, aside from showing up at the Pepperdine Stauffer Chapel. But Pepperdine was our family and our sanctuary even before Alaina was born. It was safe. It was familiar. However, we had no idea who would show up to the march. We went back and forth about it early in the morning. Heeding the advice from the Pepperdine Chaplain Sara Barton, we decided to go when we found out so many others were also planning to go. I remember thinking, *Okay, let's do this!* with one caveat. I had no desire to speak. I wanted only to participate and made that clear to Hannah. Neither one of us was prepared nor had the headspace to share any other words other than the obvious. No one from the Hero Foundation had contacted us to come or speak, but we knew they were making a well-intentioned statement to stand up against gun violence and wanted to support their mission.

Hannah, Alex, and I, with our nearest and dearest in tow, arrived near the start time at Napa's Memorial Stadium where a crowd had gathered and greeted us with many hugs and tears. It appeared the organizers were aware that we had arrived and allowed for some reception time. I was wearing a gray, blue, and orange stocking cap from Pepperdine that Alaina had won for me that summer. Even though I probably looked a bit like a clown wearing all the different colors on my head, I didn't care and was determined to wear the beanie. Alaina was so proud to have won it in a trivia contest during a reception for newly accepted Pepperdine students. It made me feel like she was with me.

After everyone greeted us and got settled, Michael Rupprecht, the founder of Hero Foundation, spoke along with a few other members. I was deeply touched by the foundation's mission and suddenly had the urge to say something. To this day, I am not sure what came over me, but the urge to speak swelled up inside me and I still wonder if it was because of the beanie, as if Alaina was there, urging me on, giving me the strength to speak the words I never thought possible after so much had hit us. I honestly didn't think I had it in me to say a word, much less break down in front of hundreds of people I had never met. I turned to Hannah and shared a knowing look, then glanced at the speaker podium. She nodded as if she already knew what I was about to do, even though we both had been staunchly opposed to saying anything public during our burrito breakfast meeting. Some force was overcoming both of us. I took Hannah's hand and together, we walked up and thanked everyone for coming.

The words fell out of my mouth. They weren't premeditated. Because I went off the cuff, I can't remember much of what I said, only that I stood grounded in my gratitude for what our community was doing, how they were showing up for us and organizing so many people to protest gun violence. Even if all they wanted to do was gather together, that would have been enough to fill both Hannah, me, and Alex with the solidarity we needed to navigate our collective sorrow. The march was one of the many showings of kindness and support from the Napa community in addition to all the food prepared for us. Looking back after Covid kept us apart for so many years, this gathering of people is still one of the greatest outpourings of compassion we received, and the first step in a million toward our collective healing. We were joined in both grief and gratiude, bonded forever by a single act of violence.

After Hannah and I spoke, many people came up to say how inspirational our words were to them and wondered how we could do it. In the beginning, all these comments were from friends. I knew they were being kind, yet as the speeches continued, many strangers approached in tears to praise our strength. Maybe this speech at the march was the catalyst to kickstart my public speaking. I don't know. I do know that if Alaina had anything to do with getting her dad outside his comfort zone, encouraging me to grow and discover new skills, she was succeeding. Every now and then, I'd reach up and adjust that colorful beanie, as if she'd been there, nudging it around, to keep me present and focused, or maybe just to remind me she would always be there with us, no matter what.

In a few short minutes, we were becoming public speakers in the midst of a media frenzy. There were camera crews and photographers at the march from the local nightly news stations. A reporter was taking pictures during the speeches, which made us all a bit uncomfortable, raising the question that would loom for years over the ethical decision to cover a story like this, versus the choice to respect those who are grieving and do what's right and kind. This particular journalist was a lot like me in that we were both bald and easy to identify. He took pictures of Lorrie and Dave's daughters,

Kate and Anie, who were known to Alaina and Alex as their "frousins" (friend-cousin). We weren't related but might as well have been. This reporter decided he would take pictures of the girls in their tears and pain. He continued to take pictures, getting progressively closer until he was within a few feet. At this point, Dave stepped in front of his daughters to shield them from this invasion. Sadly, our dear friends were feeling more violated than supported by this journalist's actions, which was the complete opposite of the Hero Foundation's intention that day. It brought me back to the time only days before when the TV cameras were swarming at the teen center. I understood they had to do their jobs, and thankfully some of them did so respectfully. I also knew that I had a new job: speaking at length about how to deal with traumatized people.

Homecoming

WHILE ALAINA MIGHT have been there in spirit during the march, we were all awaiting the return of her body. The devastating news from Borderline followed many levels of communication with Chaplain Lee, Detective Chris, and Andrea, our victims advocate from Thousand Oaks. We had been informed there would be a procession in Napa. We didn't have to do anything; we would be picked up and ushered through its entirety. This service was provided by a fund generated from a percentage of the fees and fines people pay for committing crimes. Given we were still in the throes of our trauma, we leaned into this love from our community and went with it.

It was overwhelming enough to figure out details for the burial and her memorial service, which was the perfect time to remember that it was okay to allow others to love and support us. We were navigating these mercurial waters minute by minute, and we were definitely not ready to go hunting for the burial site for our daughter. I can't imagine the burden it would have been on us, and I can only imagine how difficult this burden was for our dear friends who took this on.

Thankfully, our dear friends Lorrie and Kristi worked with a supportive team at Tulocay Cemetery. They found us a beautiful family plot on the hillside, where eventually we will lie next to Alaina. While it still felt surreal, we received word that her body was going to be released from the coroner's office in Thousand Oaks and she would be coming home the next day. A community procession was planned to take Alaina's body to the Tulocay hillside where she would be put to rest. Hannah and I were picked up by our long-time friends, Sgt. Heath of Napa Police Department and his wife Kathleen, also known to Alaina as Auntie Kay-Kay. Alex wanted to be with his soccer teammates at the final street of the procession.

Sgt. Heath and Kathleen picked us up from our house in an unmarked SUV and we headed to the Napa Sheriff's Office near the airport. On the drive to where the procession would start, Sgt. Heath informed us, "It appears Alfonso and Oscar are at the county line and she will be arriving soon."

We assumed Alaina's body had been delivered by an escort from Thousand Oaks, but Sgt. Heath told us otherwise. I asked, "Did they drive to the county line and meet them?" Heath responded, "No, they both asked for permission from Napa PD and Napa Sheriff to drive to Thousand Oaks and escort her home."

I fucking lost it and still do every time I tell this story.

Apparently, my friend Alf had asked permission of his bosses at Napa Police Department to drive down to Los Angeles and escort Alaina's body home—a twelve-hour round trip journey. Alf asked his brother Oscar, Lieutenant for the Napa Sheriff, if he knew of a deputy or someone from the Sheriff's Office who could join in bringing her home. Oscar said, "Yes. Me!" after getting permission from his boss.

Hannah and I stared at each other in disbelief and exchanged a tearful appreciation. We couldn't believe Alf and Oscar had already driven down and back with our daughter's remains. It was one of the most generous acts of kindness I had ever received.

Alfonso and I had been friends since kindergarten and he'd attended our wedding. His brother Oscar (now our Napa County Sheriff) and my brother had also been friends since early elementary school. To say we were moved by their gesture was an understatement. I was blown away when I realized that these brothers had driven down the day before and were already driving back with only three hours of rest before returning to the Sheriff's Department in Napa, where more than a hundred people, most in uniform, had gathered. Growing up in the valley, many of the uniformed officers had been lifelong friends or siblings of people I knew well. The sheriff and so many other officials were there to give us their condolences and support.

When they arrived with the black transport vehicle that carried Alaina's body, Hannah nearly collapsed at the sight of it, knowing that her daughter was inside the van.

It was like a slow-motion scene from a movie. We'd arrived only minutes before to a large number of officials, officers, and friends. When we got closer to the transport vehicle, Hannah wailed and fell into my arms where I was holding every ounce of her weight.

I don't remember hearing her cry out, I just remember the visual. I could see and feel her heartache; we took this pain together. It was the first time we had been within a close distance of Alaina's body since we left her at Pepperdine Parents Weekend in October. We were flooded with emotion, overwhelming grief, and the relief of finally having her home.

When it was time to take her body to the cemetery, we joined Heath and Kathleen in the unmarked SUV, and sat in the back seat for privacy, while our procession traveled through traffic lights without stopping. After the first two miles, I noticed people gathering at the Napa shopping center and recognized a man I knew named Anil. We had met a few times but didn't know each other well; however, when I saw him there it struck me how many others had been touched by Alaina's passing and were showing up for our family.

A few years later, I had a chance to let Anil know how much it meant to see him out there that day. He was the very first person I saw, and while there were so many familiar faces we would recognize in the procession, his face stood out. Soon, we saw more and more people gathering on the sides of Silverado Trail—one of the busiest and well-traveled roads in Napa that I had driven countless times. But that day it was different. Seeing so many people lined up shoulder to shoulder, many of whom I had never seen before, was inexplicable. They had come for us. They had come for Alaina. They had joined in our community's collective grief to show solidarity, support, and compassion. Signs and banners lined the streets reading WE LOVE YOU HOUSLEYS and ALAINA with a heart.

As we approached the final street, we turned on Coombsville Road to a sea of soccer players wearing their green Napa United training jerseys. The Director of Napa United, an Englishman named Gavin, had asked me if it was appropriate. In the UK, it's customary for people to offer a minute of applause instead of silence. When we rounded the corner, we saw Alex standing there with all his friends and teammates, hundreds of them in a sea of green. The applause roared and again I lost my shit. Hannah and I were so touched by the outpouring of love. So many friends lined the streets. We couldn't hold back the emotions. Kathleen had been an amazing support to us in the car, and I remember looking over and seeing her steady hand on Hannah's shoulder. It was such an inexplicable comfort in a moment I wish we never had to live.

Before we turned into the cemetery, we saw a woman holding a sign: "Alaina, God must have missed you more." Tears flowed yet again, and my heart ached with the loss of Alaina and this outpouring of love. It was overwhelming. After the procession, the woman had left her sign somewhere outside Tulocay and someone brought it to our house. We still have it.

By this point, the procession brought Alaina's body to the cemetery, yet her remains still needed to be cremated for a family memorial at St. Apollinaris and private graveside service, followed by a public memorial at Vintage High School, Alaina's alma mater, a few days later. We had not seen her body after the shooting and had deliberately chosen not to identify it. We wanted every memory to be of her beauty and love. It would not have made us feel any better to see her body altered in any way and conversely might have inflicted more trauma. Instead, we focused only on what we remembered—our healthy, vibrant 18-year-old daughter.

The decision came after consulting with Father Alvin Villaruel and Chaplain Lee. We needed their help in making the best decision and we trusted Father Alvin because we shared a history: He had married Hannah and me and baptized Alaina. He'd been a part of our family story for a long time. A few days after we returned home from Thousand Oaks, Father Alvin came over to see us. He wanted to discuss what we would like at the funeral and to asked us a simple question.

"In one word, how would you describe Alaina?"

I looked at Hannah; she immediately said, "Thoughtful."

When he asked why, Hannah went to the fireplace and got a little painted sign that Alaina had made. "This was the gift Alaina made for me for my birthday a couple weeks ago," she explained. The painting read: "My love, my life. You're my one and only."

They were lyrics from *Mama Mia! Here We Go Again*, the last movie Hannah and Alaina had watched together.

The song was sung by the mother, and it brought them both to tears during the movie. Alaina's birthday gift to her mother was a little reminder of that moment. She was so very thoughtful like this.

As Hannah told the story, Father Alvin looked stunned and wiped tears from his eyes.

"You're never going to believe this," he said, "but two weeks ago, I felt compelled to watch that movie. I didn't know why but I really made an effort to see it. After it was over, I wrote last week's homily on that song." We were all in tears again.

We made sound decisions to honor Alaina's life and not perpetuate her trauma. To this day, we are so grateful for the guidance we had in coming to these decisions when everything had felt so overwhelming. Some people need to see their deceased loved one. As I said before, we each do this grief journey differently, there is no right or wrong way. For me, I only wanted to see her in my mind in life—not laying lifeless on a steel table. These are healthy images and they help me sleep. My last vision of Alaina was on FaceTime where we were smiling and laughing. I am so thankful this is a piece of my reality. Her smile could light up a room and thinking of it even now brings me comfort. That is the image I want to come home to in my mind every day. This is the homecoming I will keep in my heart and the kind of choice I have made to be resilient.

Smiles in Sadness

THE UNWAVERING SUPPORT continued as dear friends came through for us every step of the way to help select the gravesite, prepare food, and coordinate travel to and from events. When it came to organizing the memorial, a kind soul and amazing friend Megan took on the role at St. Apollinaris Church, where we are parishioners. The service was as perfect as it could be considering the reason we were there. The Vintage High School Choir, with which Alaina was a member only six months prior, sounded like angels. There were definitely a lot of tears. I closed my eyes at one point, and I swear that I could hear her voice amongst the fifty members of the choir.

Due to the limited capacity for large groups to gather on the hillside gravesite, we joined only our closest family and friends there. Our friend Ryan, who was very close to Alaina, made a ceramic urn with Alaina's name and a ribbon on top. When Lorrie and Kristi went to Tulocay for the burial site selection, they had seen what the standard urns looked like, and they refused to accept that as Alaina's final resting vessel. It didn't feel right, so they asked Ryan to make something more fitting of her. I love that they took this initiative. Ryan was a year younger than Alaina and had been taught by his father to build and weld from a young age. Ryan had also learned ceramics at Vintage High School and had acquired many skills to create a beautiful urn for Alaina's remains. He also helped Alex build a special box to hold meaningful items that we would bury with her ashes. Alex decided to paint the box teal, which was Alaina's favorite color and would be the color of the bracelets we would make for the foundation in her name. The box would be placed below the urn at her burial. Prior to the service, our family and closest friends wrote words on rocks that meant something to Alaina: *love, sister, frousin, cousin, hope,* and whatever was important to them. Included was a note to Alaina to be put in the box with some special items—her favorite bracelets, an ENOUGH T-shirt, a letter from a cousin, and, of course, a container of dark chocolate powder from Coffee Bean and Tea Leaf.

    We'd bury these items with her ashes. At the end of her service, we'd each toss a handful of dirt over the urn. As Alex and I walked up, we grabbed a fistful to deposit over the site. When we let go, rather than the sound of dirt falling on the ceramic, we heard a *clink* and saw that the delicate ribbon on the urn Ryan had made of thin porcelain had been broken by a small but formidable rock. We froze, staring at each other, wondering whose fistful of dirt had the rock.

It was one of those awkward moments when emotions collide. Horror and humor struck us right then and we murmured a giggle. We never imagined ourselves in that moment, hoping that everything was "perfect" but suddenly wondering if anyone happened to have some Super Glue in their pocket or purse. Because let's face it, it seemed like a reasonable item to bring to Alaina's burial. Knowing her sense of humor, we sensed she might be in on the joke, too, just to keep things a wee lighter. Although nobody else knew what happened, we glanced over at Hannah who shared a knowing look. Our family had always shared a level of communication outside the norm. Laughter had always bonded us. When we sat back down, I whispered to Hannah what had happened and we exchanged a tearful smile. Our Housley humor had rescued us in this moment of inexplicable anguish. It is hard to explain the bond that the three of us share after what we've been through, but it allows us to laugh and cry with ease. These were the kind of moments that brought us one of many smiles in our sadness. To this day, Alex and I still like to tease each other about which one of us dropped the rock that broke the ceramic ribbon.

We would need humor to carry us through the next service at her high school. Slow-forward two days to the memorial in the Vintage High School gym, where more than a thousand people would gather. The timing was unbelievable, as it nearly marked the one-year anniversary when we were there for the memorial of two other dear friends, Daryl and Joe Horn, who had died in a car accident with two other family members. Now we were there for Alaina; it was surreal hearing so many young people speak about her. Our nineteen-year-old niece, Moorea, eloquently described growing up with her reading buddy. Then Alaina's best friends, Anie and Kate, shared stories of their deep friendship with Alaina and others recounted wonderful memories that meant so much to us. We felt pride, sorrow and joy all at once.

One of her friends, Jack, shared a moment in which he recalled sitting on a bench at Vintage High School when Alaina noticed he was feeling particularly down one day. She introduced herself and asked him to join her and her friends at recess, and a forever friendship was born. We heard similar accounts from her friends at Pepperdine. Alaina could make a stranger feel the embrace of her kindness—a theme that would become her legacy.

When it came time for Alex to speak, I remember feeling a combination of nervousness and pride. Here was our son who had for years shied away from the spotlight and was not the most gregarious person or a contender for public speaking, but he looked poised, even calm in the midst of our circumstances. He stood firmly rooted with the eulogy in his hand, as resolved as he had been the morning he learned that Alaina had been murdered. Without asking him or even considering it might be something he might do some day, he wrote the eulogy, alone, in a hotel room—tasking me with the same kind of courage I was not sure I had. He had shown me then how capable he was, but nothing prepared me for what he demonstrated that day. He was fourteen but behaving like a forty-year-old. Who was the father? I questioned if it was me that day.

Alex Ernesto Housley was born April 1, 2004, an Aries and April Fool's birthday baby. He would be our quiet fire from the start—not one to be pushed into doing anything but the kind of person who forges their own path when it feels right. From an early age, Alex was very intuitive but not very talkative. My parents were worried because he hardly spoke until the age of two. My dad asked if he needed to see a speech specialist. I told him, "Why does he need to speak when he has his sister, the interpreter?" Over the years, Alex would show us that he was always happy to just listen and learn. He had no need to suck the life out of the room; instead, he just sensed it. He had always been very curious and ready to learn—with extremely quick wit.

His intuition was duly noted when Hannah came home one day from the salon after getting her hair done. We were sitting at the table and Alex looked over at Hannah and said, "Your hair looks nice, Mom." Hannah looked at me and exchanged a knowing look. In the twenty years I had known her, I rarely if ever noticed these kinds of things. But my son? Dammit kid! I was over forty years old but never realized that simple statement was so powerful. Hannah was delighted to receive this compliment from her son. At least one male in her house showed signs of promise.

Alex would teach me a few things from his playbook over the years about his quiet superpower of observation, at least of the females in his life. From the moment he was born, he had a wonderful big sister in Alaina, whom Alex later nicknamed his "second mom." He looked up to her in every way, and when I began coaching her soccer team, he started to show up at the game in a full kit ready to join her. Why? He had observed us and while he might not have been saying much, he knew a ton. He knew I loved soccer and soccer meant love. It also meant love for his sister, which meant love for him. So he showed up, ready to play too. In our favorite picture of him, he's sporting an England uniform with Adidas samba shoes, socks pulled up and ready to go. He has his leg lifted high to hoist his little foot on top of the soccer ball, stretching to reach it because he was so small next to the huge ball. It didn't matter to Alex. He already knew he would grow up one day and fit it all—from his uniform to his rightful place on the field.

On the day of Alaina's service, Alex walked slowly, proudly, and absolutely prepared. It didn't surprise me that he was ready to read her eulogy a week before the service. Alex was always methodical in his ways and a creature of habit. Prior to a soccer game, he would have his uniform laid out with no wrinkles and bag ready the night before. He went to bed early for a good night's sleep and always made his bed and sorted things the next morning before he opened his door. This is how Alex greeted life. That day, seeing him in the gymnasium, I realized it was the way he also greeted death.

What would happen next continues to fill Hannah and me with awe. Remember, Alex was not a talker, let alone a public speaker, so we were reasonably nervous, yet hopeful, based on Alex's history. When he was a toddler, he split his head open on a vacation in Mexico. While he had been a curious kid, always smiling and ready for fun, things suddenly changed. He immediately showed signs of being cautious and carried a sense of anxiety for years. When he was only ten years old, an earthquake rattled Napa County and heavily hit our two grocery stores that I owned and operated. My brother was with Fox News at the time and requested our stores' security footage to share all over national news that showed all the items falling off our shelves. It didn't help our son recover from the earthquake, and he worried about us getting hurt in other earthquakes that had not happened yet. Alex's anxiety was only heightened during the 2014 earthquake.

The next year, we had a small kitchen fire. Both Alex and Alaina had friends over to spend the night when this incident happened that would only keep him in his anxiety loop. I had gone to bed and Hannah was still putting away laundry in the bedroom. She woke me and said, "Arik, what is that noise?" There was a high-pitched beeping in the distance. I sat up listening to the sound, trying to figure out where it was coming from, thinking it was in our bedroom. "Probably the TV," I said. She paused the TV, but the noise continued. Then we heard a knock on the door. Little Alex and Lucas were standing in the hall, both about four feet tall. Just above their heads was a cloud of smoke on the ceiling. Something was burning.

"Hannah, get them out of the house!" I yelled.

Hannah grabbed the boys and took Alaina and her friend outside. I sprinted down the hallway through the house to get the extinguisher and find the fire, forgetting to duck down low. Instead, I ran out the front door heaving and coughing for air. After a few clean breaths, I ran back into the house, got lower and grabbed the fire extinguisher from the kitchen, where the fire was burning. I pulled the pin and moved into the living room instead to test it first. I pulled the trigger, and powder flew all over the rug and couch while the fire kept burning in our kitchen.

Frustrated, and in disbelief that I was so disoriented to make this mistake, I went back into the kitchen and used it to put out the fire. I was surprised to discover that our Bosch dishwasher's digital display had combusted and was on fire—burning the whole kitchen. I was quickly able to extinguish it. While we opened the doors and windows to clear the smoke, we called a firefighter friend who suggested we call the fire department to make sure everything was safe to stay in the house. The firefighters arrived and checked everything, telling me, "A couple more minutes, and this would have been unstoppable with the heat. You're lucky you caught it when you did."

Although Hannah and the kids were safely outside, so many questions arose from Alex's anxiety after this incident. "Dad, will there be another earthquake? Dad, what if we get in a car accident? Dad, am I going to be okay if I get sick?" One day, after witnessing one of his friend's being bullied at school, he asked me on our drive home, "Dad, am I gay?"

Curious, I turned to him. "I don't know, Alex, why do you ask?"

He explained that some of the kids were calling his friend names he didn't think were nice. "He's my friend and he recently told people he was gay," he said. I turned to Alex again. "Alex, we love you no matter what. But just because you have a friend that is gay doesn't make you the same." But in the event my son was trying to tell me something else, I continued. "Do you have feelings for a boy?"

"No," he said.

"Do you have feelings for a girl?"

"No," he said, looking at me with his big eyes.

I said, "Look, you are in seventh grade, you don't have to worry about this stuff, but I am proud of you for standing up to your friends on his behalf."

Over the years, despite my reassurances, Alex had some anxiety and needed help to know how to differentiate between a real threat versus a perceived one. We took Alex to see a child therapist, Dr. Dan, who was amazing. After only a couple sessions, Alex had acquired tools to deal with the anxiety he was facing. Dr. Dan explained that anxiety is fear of the future and what hasn't yet happened, and depression is sorrow about things in the past. Alex understood that it's futile to worry about what hasn't yet happened, because it hasn't happened and it might not.

Several years later, it was Alex who would remain calm in the face of the tragic Tubbs Fire of October 2017 that started near where we live in Napa. Little did he know that a year later, his sister would be deceased. When the fires began, he remained strong minded, remembering the therapist's words. *Anxiety is fear of the future that hasn't happened yet.*

After tending to our family and making sure we were okay, I drove a mile to my parents to see their situation, as they lived on the eastern edge of the hills of Napa Valley. After making trips back and forth to my parents and our house, the Tubbs Fire was getting worse, and I realized it was time to evacuate my folks. While Grandma came to our house to be further away from the fire, Grandpa grabbed his garden hose, ready to fight it. If you saw the immense wall of flames coming toward their home, you can only imagine what was going through my head seeing my father gripping that hose like he was taking his BB gun to the Vietnam War. Yet he would stand defiant in the face of the flames, refusing to let his house burn.

By the time I got back to our house, seeing embers the size of golf balls dropping on our lawn, I told Hannah it was time for her, the kids, and Grandma to hightail it out of there. She was ready and told us she would drive Grandma and Grandpa's car, but she needed Alaina to drive Hannah's car. When Alaina showed a bit of apprehension, it was Alex, only thirteen then, who assured her that she could do it. He rode in the front seat, calming her down so that she could drive them out of the scary moment. He told her it would be okay and encouraged her to continue despite her fear. Just as he would tell her in the eulogy he wrote that fateful November night in 2018:

Alaina Maria Housley
July 27, 2000—November 7, 2018

Alaina Housley, as most of you know, was my sister but I liked to call her my second mom. There would be no other sister in the world who could replace her. Alaina was a big help to my academic success whether it was advice on projects or helping me with math homework that I really didn't get. Sometimes I would ask her for help and then she would talk for a while and all I would respond with was "u-huh" or "okay." Although she talked a lot, she was a very good listener, when she wanted to be. She would always want to know about the drama going on at my school or who was dating who. I've heard all these things about her bragging about me and it was hard to believe because I would get on her nerves so much by just knocking on her door and then hiding around the corner, she would get so mad. Another thing I would do is eat her food, which I didn't know was hers, and then she would try to make me feel bad even though I didn't know that it was her food. If there was one thing I could have said to my sister before she left it would be, "Thank you for all you did for me. I couldn't have asked for a better sister." These next few weeks, months, and years are going to be difficult for all of us. A man I met in Los Angeles just last week said to tell stories, and my task for all of you is to share stories about Alaina with anyone and it will truly help all the grief. I would also like everyone to be kind to each other and spend time with your loved ones. My family and I really appreciate all the support that you guys have been providing. It is really cool to see all these strangers wishing the best to my family and me as well as all the little things like the JC soccer team wearing black tape over their wrists with "Alaina" on it. Thank you.

I am not sure if we were in tears of sorrow or pride listening to him speak. He made us laugh with his reference to Alaina as his "second mom" and he made us cry with his sincerity and love for her. It still brings tears to my eyes seeing it on paper.

When it came time for Hannah and me to speak, we got so much love and energy from the room. Many people ask us how we could do it and my response is almost always the same. We could do it because people showed up for us. We could do it because we were not alone. We could do it because it was larger than us and it was the right thing to do, to honor our daughter. The love and support of our community wrapped its arms around us when we most needed it.

The night in the hotel room when Alex closed his laptop and told me he had written his speech, I knew there was another piece to it. I still don't understand what unfolded next. I just remember walking next door to Hannah's parents' room to tell them I was going to bed. When I returned to our hotel room, I pulled out my phone and began writing in my notes app. Eight minutes later, I finished my eulogy. It felt as if someone was speaking through my fingertips. I don't understand how it happened, and when I shared it with some close friends, they said to leave it exactly like I wrote it. While it was raw, with many grammatical errors, it resonated with them, so I read it right there at Vintage High School, where my wife worked as a teacher, where Alaina and I had graduated and where Alex was in his first year as a freshman.

Hug your friends even if the same gender, it's not gay.
It's okay to be gay.
It's okay to be you.
It's okay to be me.
It's okay to be fat or skinny or short or tall,
it's even okay to be bald trust me . . .

It's okay to own guns, but let's not use them on others.
It's okay to worship Allah, Buddha, Jesus,
or whomever if you choose.
It's okay to be different.
It's okay to be the same.

Do your best at all times, even though sometimes
your best may be 50 percent.
Do what is right when no one is looking. It will all work out.
Do not worry you aren't good enough. If you give your best
and they aren't happy then it's not meant to be.
Do not blame others, you make your destiny.

Alaina Housley had a destiny to change the world. Her life may have ended but her legacy will not die as long as I am alive.

My daughter lived, laughed, and loved.
She loved Vintage, Pepperdine, her family, her friends.
She loved old movies. She loved milk, and musicals.
She loved music and chocolate as long as it was dark, of course.
She loved to talk, watch Friends, read, read, and read some more.
She read more in one weekend than I did in my entire high school and college careers combined.

ALWAYS NOVEMBER | Arik Housley

We must love one another.
We must respect our differences.
We must appreciate that we are not the same,
for example if your only choice was always vanilla ice cream
then ice cream would not be that awesome.

We must end senseless acts of violence because they are just that.
Senseless.
We must believe the world is mostly good.

We must know that every police officer is a brother or sister,
friend, and family member and while they are human and make
mistakes, they show up to work knowing they may have to put
their life on the line. They are never allowed to give 50 percent
at work but you are. Respect the difficulty of the work they do.

Put your phone down and look out the window.
Wait on that text message, it's not worth someone's life
including your own.
Parents, talk to your children during dinner
rather than have them think or feel your phone
is more important than they are.
Children, talk to your parents
for the exact same reason.
Take a break and just be in the present.

A beautiful woman passed as did eleven others
in Thousand Oaks in a senseless act of violence.
If the shooter had mental support would that have happened?
What about Parkland, Las Vegas, Yountville?

To the media: Sadly, I remember two names from Columbine, Dylan and Erik.
Stop posting the names. Unless they are the victim.
Stop sensationalizing.
To the government and our political officials:
If you can cut off my live feed for playing "Thriller" at an elementary school and silence it, you can make sure postings showing these senseless acts of violence are silenced. It's not censorship, it's the right thing to do.

I took a deep breath, feeling the rush of emotions. It was hard to believe I had actually just said all that. I could also feel the anger coursing through me with regard to the "Thriller" comment. I had done a live feed at a school event where "Thriller" was playing in the background. Facebook cut my post, telling us we could not play the song publicly without permission, and yet they could allow a shooter to go live with heinous acts. It incensed me and still does. My body trembled as I stood there, feeling this mix of emotion. I had said everything I needed to say. Although I would have never conceived the extent to which Alaina's murder would call on me to speak publicly about grief and resilience, I had been asked to speak throughout my life since I was in fifth grade, which helped me get past my initial fear. Now, I feel compelled to share what I know even if it means just one more person feels less alone in their grief process, especially when so many struggle to discuss it.

When I see people I have never met before so moved from our story of resilience, it inspires me to keep speaking.

I am motivated to help others. That said, it was hard to fathom that I was the person speaking at my child's funeral. Before this experience, I would not have thought it was possible to stand before so many people and show such vulnerability. However, when I stood next to Alex and Hannah, looking at a sea of people overflowing from one room to the next, I felt so much love and sorrow simultaneously. It was a feeling I wish no parent ever has to experience, yet it was amazing at the same time, and it was the only reason we could survive our grief. We had a community buoying us. It made me realize if we all were more supportive of one another in times of deep sorrow and loss, it was possible that together we could save one more life, stop one more shooting, and help one more person to make this world a better place. Anything was possible if we could find a way to keep smiling through our sadness.

Four years later, when it was time for Alex to graduate from high school, he mentioned wanting to try out to be a commencement speaker. As the token public speaker of our family, I was intrigued and asked him why. He explained it would be "cool to do something different."

A few weeks later, he suddenly seemed apprehensive. We had always joked with Alex about nicknaming him Mr. Changer-Minder. When I asked him why he wasn't going to try, he said he didn't know what to say. I realized he hadn't gotten his bearings on what he wanted to say or how he could talk about his own experience with grief. My heart broke for him, because I sensed he had so much he wanted to say but had not been able to untangle the knots in his head.

I told him, "Alex, most of these speeches are an attempt to inspire. Many are long winded and are just about the speaker. Your generation is obsessed with selfies and their number of likes. Why don't you give a speech about what you've learned from your classmates?"

Alex flashed a smile. I could see his wheels turning.

"Give me one person you look up to."

"Gabey Baby!" Alex said, naming his long-time friend from soccer who exuded such great energy. I said, "Perfect. Now see if you can get two more guys and maybe two to four girls who inspired you. The stories don't need to be long."

That was all it took for Alex to write his speech.

Graduation day came, post-COVID-19, so we had family in tow while others were able to watch the graduation on Zoom. Luckily, I had my sunglasses to cover my tears of pride because Alex hadn't shared one piece. When he was called to speak, he appeared to unzip his graduation robe. I sat up straight, wondering what he was going to do next. If my son wasn't a rule follower, I would have been worried about what was under the robe.

Alex delivered his speech, acknowledging many of his classmates for their resilience, drive, kindness, and friendship, much to his classmates' delight. After the ceremony was over, many of his friends who had streamed were sharing comments. "It was so cool what Alex did." I thought they were speaking about his speech in general, but they were referring to the fact that when Alex unzipped his robe, he was wearing his Napa Valley 1839 ENOUGH jersey. This special jersey was produced in 2019 to commemorate the twelve people who lost their lives including Alaina at Borderline in November 2018, three women murdered at the Yountville veterans' Pathway Home of California in March 2018, and the fifty-four cities that had mass shootings between January 2017 and August 2019, the same timeframe that the Napa Valley soccer team we own had been in existence. It was my idea and created by designer Chris Payne.

When Alex unzipped his robe, he included everyone who had been affected by multiple mass shootings, not just those from Borderline. His inclusivity and turning the focus away from his particular story to how others inspired him in the midst of his grief was what brought down the house. He wasn't speaking about living through unimaginable tragedy. He spoke about how others had uplifted him during that incident and how he celebrated their support. I could not have been more touched and inspired. Rather than take pity on him, which he did not want, anyone listening was inspired to take action. Everyone can make a difference in the life of another. Kindness matters. Alex's speech turned out to be the ultimate testimony to the power of smiling through sadness.

Calm After the Storm

I REMEMBER THE following Sunday, ten days after we lost Alaina, when everyone was heading back to their normal lives. I felt nervous. I had no idea what tomorrow looked like, but I was trying to figure out how I would head back to work. How would I act, feel, or function day to day?

Our new life of grieving had been filled with a lot of activity: planning, feeding, speaking, hugging, and crying. We were not prepared for the two weeks that followed, when everyone disappeared. While we continued to receive messages and other communication, the utter craziness turned into a disturbing degree of quiet. We went from traveling, processions, meetings at the cemetery, a march against gun violence, memorials, a funeral, and then to what seemed like nothing. The most challenging time was saying goodbye to all the friends and family who had made the trip to support us. One of my closest friends, Levi, who had flown out from New Jersey, came over one morning with a surprise.

As we stood in my driveway, I expected him to hug me goodbye because he had to get back to his family, but he had made other plans.

"When do you have to head out?" I asked.

"I thought you might want to hang out, so I'm here for the week," he said.

I was stunned. I figured he would have to head back to the East Coast immediately, given the time he had already spent with us. Choosing to stay was a gesture I could never have imagined someone making, and it was incredibly meaningful. I needed him there more than I could admit. He knew it, and I didn't even realize how much I needed it until after he was gone. I loved him for sensing this was exactly what I needed. We just stood there in the driveway, sharing a knowing look followed by a big thankful hug.

"Of course I'm staying," he said. And that was that.

We had a lot of great laughs during those few days after everyone else had gone. He even volunteered as a parking lot attendant at our Napa Valley 1839 FC game. Levi was rolling with all of this and was such a good sport, but when I noticed tears welling up in his eyes one day, I wondered what might have gone wrong. We were in the house with our two chocolate labs named Kahlua and Corona and I wasn't sure what had overcome Levi. I turned to him, concerned. "Levi, what's up? You okay?"

He rubbed his swollen eyes and finally confessed. "I am really allergic to dogs!"

"What the hell?" I said. "You've been here for days and didn't say a thing!"

He just looked at me with his watery red eyes and smiled in spite of his misery.

"Dude," I said, in disbelief.

Levi shook his head and sneezed.

We immediately vacated the living room where the dogs were hanging out. About an hour later, Hannah walked into the master bedroom (where the dogs weren't allowed) to find Levi and me on the bed, talking and watching TV. The look on her face seeing us there was priceless. Of course, there were many inappropriate comments from us boys to let Hannah know she had competition. Especially given the red puffy eyes like we'd had a good long cry. When we let her in on Levi's allergy, we all burst out laughing. Levi's sense of humor, even in the midst of such tragedy, was a buoy that I will never forget. To feel something other than pain was a gift I didn't know I needed to keep me breathing each day. At another point during Levi's stay, I remember Hannah coming into the master bedroom where Levi and I were watching a movie and beaming a smile, seeing us like brothers, the way she once saw us in college.

Levi's decision to stay was one of the greatest gifts we could have ever received at the time. To this day, I share his story with so many others as an example of one of the best acts of kindness anyone can take for those facing such devastation. The challenge for most people who are in a cycle of trauma is that they are so flooded by emotion they are not able to think about what they need. I had no idea what I needed. I didn't know what to ask for. This is not because I didn't have needs. I had a ton of needs but didn't have language around them because my mind was so caught up in the reality of our new normal. Even if I could articulate a need, I didn't want to ask. For those who have grieved, sound familiar? My situation was no different from anyone else who has lost a loved one, especially if the loss was sudden or unexpected.

I'm so grateful that Levi sensed what I needed and gave it to me before I could even ask or *knew* to ask. If he had said, "Arik, if there's anything I can do, will you please let me know?" I would not have answered. Many people have shared the same response. The grief-stricken and traumatized are not in a place to be proactive. Trauma renders us reactive. It's our human nature to protect ourselves instinctively in those moments but we are not wired to plan or even think logically. I would have never thought of asking him to stay or even consider that he or anyone else would or could take that time. The best advice I can offer is to help the person who is traumatized by making good decisions on their behalf. Be proactive. Don't just offer because as much as you might mean it, 99 percent of the time, those in grief won't be able to ask or answer.

When a family is dealing with loss, any loss, it is a lot to bear. At first there might be people and food everywhere. There is so much love and support in your home with so many people constantly around. All of a sudden, it shifts from little to nothing. We still had interspersed events and recognitions for Alaina and our family throughout the year. What we did not know to prepare for was the new silence and emptiness we started to feel. For some people, the calm after the storm is momentarily beautiful, quiet, and peaceful; to others it is lonely, sad, and extremely difficult. One of the best practices anyone can do to support someone in grief is to check in from time to time, and not just on expected days, like the anniversary of the loss. When Hannah and I were first married, she wisely requested, "Don't buy me flowers on Valentine's Day just because it feels like you're supposed to. It's really expensive for no reason at that time of year. Buy me flowers, just because, when I am not expecting it."

The best thing anyone can do for another on their grief journey is to be like Levi and give when the other person is least expecting it. Or like Lorrie, who came over a month after Alaina's passing to be with Hannah when I was away at a conference. Kindness really matters and is a mighty medicine for healing grief. Thankfully, we were about to receive more of it in Malibu.

With the Woolsey Fire finally extinguished, we returned to Pepperdine for Alaina's final memorial shortly after Thanksgiving. We found comfort in the chaplain's advice to be present in each moment. We heeded his wisdom so that we had enough energy for not just one memorial, but two. We were barely home two weeks and trying to assimilate into our new reality when we had to return to the last place we left her when she was alive. At first, we just hoped to get it over with and schedule the services back to back, but because of the fires and holiday, the service in Pepperdine was a few weeks later. We didn't resist and just went with the flow, finding our way—moment by moment—the only way that the brain can manage when it's traumatized.

Despite the flood of emotions, we found deep comfort at Pepperdine, thanks to the generosity of Dr. Andrew K. Benton, the president at the time, and his team. They were extremely kind at every turn and provided us with housing at their Broad Beach property. The sound of the waves crashing below the house was very calming and helped ease our nervous systems. With this reset, we were able to say yes to a few unexpected opportunities and reconnect with friends, family, and Alaina's suitemates, who came over for brunch. We had time to visit and share funny stories, laugh and cry.

It was all a bit surreal at first when we entered the Tyler Campus Center, where the bookstore, cafeteria, and some student service offices are located. We stood in the hallway of the upper floor, seeing the girls. The tension was palpable. We could sense they were uncomfortable to be near us. It was the first time we had all seen each other since Parents Weekend. Understandably, I wasn't sure how comfortable I would be either. The irony also wasn't lost on me that we were standing in a newly renovated meeting room close to the Student Government Office where Hannah and I had met over twenty-five years earlier. Later, our dear friend Hung told us how amazed he was seeing us ministering to Alaina's suitemates that day. We had unknowingly taken on the role to guide and nurture these special young ladies who shared a joyful relationship with our daughter and to this day still share with us.

All these moments provided us with a path forward—not by closing the doors to anything associated with Pepperdine because of our grief, but conversely opening our world in ways we never could have imagined. Detective Chris, who served as a member of the search and rescue team, gave us the opportunity to ride in a helicopter during some downtime. Alex was unbelievably excited when the day came for us to load up from Broad Beach and head to Camarillo to get the helicopter. Hannah stayed on the beach with her sister Theresa and our dear friend Jeneen, Alaina's "spiritual godmother" who was living in the area. Janeen was a devout Christian who was getting her advanced degree in religious studies, and we felt the nickname fit. It felt good to have her watching us—and sending blessings for our helicopter ride.

The search and rescue team showed us what they do and gave us an insiders' look at the helicopter and their equipment. None of us had ever been up in a helicopter and the thrill did wonders to shift our whole being—bringing a moment of much-needed joy to everyone watching and for those taking the ride. With our headsets on, we flew over the hills of Malibu toward the Pacific Ocean and got close enough to where Hannah and the ladies could see us from Broad Beach. I caught the look on Alex, Zac, and Moorea's faces and knew this was a gift. They were smiling. I got choked up, knowing how much tragedy we had all been through together.

Here's the miracle. Flying in the helicopter for a short ride enabled them to feel joy in the midst of their despair.

I knew then that this was one of the odd implications of enduring tragedy. Most people don't understand that joy and despair can co-exist, and it was moments like this that helped us move forward—without fear for the first time. Life would take, but it would also give. In our darkness, we could also see light. In the vast cerulean waters of the Pacific, we were given this expansive view of life's greatest oxymoron. We were flying above our sorrow yet carrying it with us. We were grieving yet we were glad. We were a mix of emotions flying for one blessed moment in that sky—and perhaps just a little closer to where Alaina's spirit resided.

I could never thank Detective Chris enough for all the little moments he was there for my family. It helped us to be that much more present for the last service at Pepperdine and a few other events that were so thoughtfully organized and showed so much love and respect for our daughter and the others affected by her murder. The memorial service gathered a full house at Firestone Fieldhouse on campus. After the helicopter ride and my new perspective, I felt more grounded when it came time for me to speak. Strangely and very mysteriously, each of these events was forcing me into a public speaking role—something I would have never imagined, but clearly Alaina was fully orchestrating for her dad to keep growing and showing up for her. So I stood and pulled up the notes on my phone to read what I had finally written for her—inspired by my son's initiative in first writing his words the very night he learned of her death. I read:

Part One | THE UNTHINKABLE | 99

Alaina's mother Hannah and I would first like to thank everyone for the wonderful messages received. The art, letters, scripture passages, especially the hugs and smiles.

Destiny brought Hannah and me to this university. Hannah and I met here at Pepperdine in 1994. She applied to multiple universities. I, on the other hand, only applied to Pepperdine.

I entered Payson Library as a high school freshman and saw two very hot girls sitting behind the desk, and I was sold. Many didn't believe I only applied to one university. No way would I get accepted now, but things happen for a reason.

Pepperdine was where we made some unbelievable friendships, had experiences abroad for Hannah in London and me in Florence. Experiences for me like getting salmonella poisoning in Florence, dorm golf with Dorm 2 (still don't know the house name), SongFest, and starting a fraternity because hazing was and still is unacceptable.

Pepperdine changed my life for the better. I learned to live with respect for other cultures, other ethnicities, other religions, and other political views. I learned that I am the only one who stands in my way.

Alaina loved Pepperdine. She loved her suitemates and her roommate. She loved to sing, play piano and ukulele. She loved to be funny even though it didn't come as often as she'd prefer. She was upset when she didn't get the sorority she thought she wanted but I told her life happens for a reason and to trust God has a plan. Not long after, she was accepted to the Florence program and the mock trial team; with both she was unbelievably excited.

Life happens for a reason.
She loved Coffee Bean's "Dark Chocolate Ice Blended." She loved milk and she loved to read. According to her suitemates, they didn't understand how she was done studying and would score so well after watching a Netflix marathon the night before an exam. Alaina got her intellect from her mother because if you ask Dr. Caldwell, Dr. Sexton, or any of my other professors who are still teaching, I wasn't that kind of student. Trust me, I married up.

Life happens for a reason.
Alaina was so happy; she was only unhappy if one of the girls wouldn't drive her to Coffee Bean at specific times. She called to tell me, "Did you know Uber Eats won't deliver from Coffee Bean?"

November 7, Alaina finished her homework, as well as her mock trial work she needed to do. She was invited to go line dancing at a place we would go back to when Hannah and I went here. We encouraged her, and we would do it ALL AGAIN. We would encourage her to go to Pepperdine, to try new things, and to go line dancing because He has a plan.

A man with some sort of mental illness walked into a bar and in the process killed twelve people before taking his own life. Our government should do more background checks before taking people into the military, teaching them to be trained killers, and then trying to get them to acclimate back into society.

Our media shouldn't print the names of these perpetrators or show their pictures to give them their fifteen minutes of fame. Tell the story, but don't make them celebrities.

Hannah, Alex, and I are sad, and we have a gaping hole inside that will never be filled, but Alaina was happy, she was loved, and she is a part of His plan.

Because LIFE happens for a reason.
There are many people around us who need help. Put down your phone and make eye contact with someone. Have a conversation with your friends and loved ones. Meet someone new each day. Say hello to a stranger. Buy someone "Dark Chocolate Ice Blended" from Coffee Bean so they don't have to call Uber eats and get denied. You will be surprised how far a smile can go to change someone's day. If someone is alone, strike up a conversation.
Enjoy this wonderful university you are at. Be in the moment and if nothing else, BE KIND.

I looked up to a room full of people who had received those words and were wiping tears from their eyes, just like me. I drew in a deep breath, seeing the faces of so many people who loved our daughter, who loved us, and who loved Pepperdine. In that moment, we had become one enormous family, bonded forever by this tragedy that was inadvertently bringing so much beauty into our lives. If everyone standing in that room carried Alaina in their hearts, the love for her and her love for them was radiating beyond campus, beyond the confines of those California hills, and would continue for years. I felt complete. The words had come through me, but were not of me, and they were just right for now.

After the speech, we had time for hugs and conversations before packing our stuff and making the trek back to Napa. We had reunited with so many amazing individuals, but it was time to head back to the real world, this time on a commercial airline—Southwest.

    Before we left, we had one last pickup. All of Alaina's belongings had been boxed and were ready for shipping. We asked if her suitemates wanted any of her clothing because Alaina loved to find a good sale. The only piece I remember was a leather jacket that Ashley wanted. It meant a lot to us that the girls wanted a small piece of Alaina to take with them as a reminder that while she was no longer with us in body, she would always be with us in spirit.

Signs

IN THE DAYS, weeks, and years that followed our homecoming, my life started to take on curious events. Things were happening that I could not explain and, at times, had a hard time understanding. In my search for faith, I had always struggled. I was a data driven person, in search of the tangible. The measurable. The obvious. Subtlety was not something I noticed, but something was at work to make me see the signs. Maybe you can call it *déjà vu*, which I've experienced only a few times in my life, though I could never understand how it happened—or what exactly *was* happening.

One such moment happened in September 2022, four years after Alaina's passing. We were in York, England, at an Airbnb and had made friends with the owners. I remembered them immediately because one year prior to meeting them, they showed up in a dream. Hannah and I were sitting in a kitchen, with two people I had never met. I could describe what they looked like and what they were wearing, but they weren't familiar to me.

When I awoke, I remember wondering, *Who are these people and where am I?* Yet when taking Alex to university in York, England, I found Hannah and myself standing around the kitchen island of their home. It was the same kitchen from my dream and they were wearing what I saw in the dream. I pondered, *What the hell is going on? How is this real?* I was already here. I rarely if ever remembered details or moments in a dream, but I could recall it all vividly. This whole thing kind of freaked me out. It was weird and wild but true.

When we got back to the Airbnb, I had to tell Hannah about my dream. She knows I am not one to make up stories, especially something like this. What I had just experienced was unsettling. Even though she had never experienced anything like it, I knew deep down she believed me.

It wasn't the first time it had happened either. A year prior, I had a dream where I sat in a room with our dear friend Andy and a woman I didn't know. It was a random vision that went unnoticed. The next day, we left York and returned to London. When we walked into a pub with our friends Andy and Laura, I suddenly remembered seeing Hannah and Alex on the bench seats there from the different dream. It was completely wild. I stood there, stunned, making the connection, feeling disoriented in the pub.

Was I really there this time, or still in my dream?

When our friends waved us over, I knew I was there in real time but could not shake the odd *déjà vu*. I've had this happen in the past, but never like this, two days in a row. What was going on? When we returned to the hotel after dinner, Hannah was also very curious about what happened. All I could share were the details from these odd visions. What did it all mean? I wasn't sure, but I was experiencing these things more frequently ever since Alaina's death.

One of the first signs I received was shortly after her burial. Twelve days later, November 19, 2018, I decided I would visit Alaina's gravesite for the first time by myself. Until that time, we had been surrounded by so much love and support from family and friends. Now, we were adjusting to our day-to-day life without Alaina and everyone else for long periods of time. Usually, I am a very extroverted person and am not sure why I felt compelled to go on my own that day, but I did. I was doing a lot of new things—guided by an odd inner tug.

As I weaved my way through the little streets of the cemetery, I listening to Sirius XM radio and felt the emptiness in my chest. I missed Alaina deeply. I started my ascent up the last little hill towards the site and my radio switched to music on my phone through the car audio. All of a sudden, "Amazing Grace" came on. And not just at the same volume either. It was as if someone had blasted the volume, cranking it up from level three to nine.

It was so loud it startled me. This was a song I sang at times and remembered a great version I'd heard at Pepperdine, twenty-five years prior, performed by an acapella group, named, of course, Acapella. This was the same group. Same song. Only playing super loud, which made me jump. To say the hairs were raised on my neck and arms is an understatement. I gripped the steering wheel as I approached Alaina's gravesite, wondering what the heck was going on.

This was my first unusual experience, but it would not be my last.

Later that month, Hannah and I saw advertisements for a new show on television called *God Friended Me*. We both gave each other a look of curiosity, wondering if the show would be good, yet I remember one of us saying we weren't convinced. Were they trying to reenact the Michael Landon series concept of the 80s? We weren't sure but we were compelled to find out.

Hannah and I hadn't watched much TV since Alaina's murder because there was, and continues to be, so much violence and darkness on that medium that remind us of the shadow side of humanity. We looked for more hopeful and inspiring programming. A few days later, I was flipping through the channels and discovered *God Friended Me*, which had been airing for a few months. In that episode, the character was speaking of a girl who had lost her mom. The girl's name was Hannah. This caught my attention. I gave my wife a curious look, aware she could tell what was going through my head. "Did they just say Hannah and talk about losing her?"

With goosebumps, we agreed to watch the show from the beginning. The thought that I turned it on exactly starting at the statement with the names stopped me cold. Later, I found myself speechless during a scene where a minister says to his son, "Faith is not just about religion, faith is about believing in what you are doing. Faith is the people whom you are helping. Faith is your friendships. Faith is your belief that you are making a difference in the world, no matter what people think or how crazy it seems."

I looked at Hannah with tears in my eyes. She had always been a person of faith and it buoyed us. We were very aware that we were supposed to watch this episode. It could not have been more perfect right then. As it turned out, I was living this articulation and could no longer deny that I had also become a person of faith. I could see it in her eyes; Hannah knew something had clicked for me. I finally got it. I understood faith. We now call these "God moments."

The signs continued. One day, a stranger contacted me via Facebook Messenger. It was November 16, 2018. Her message read: "Sorry to bother you in this difficult moment and sorry for the weird question I'm about to ask you. Do you guys have a dog? I had a dream with your daughter and there was one boy and you in the dream. I don't know your family. I just know the tragic situation. I'm very sorry. But my message to you and your family is that she is okay. She is very happy with what you and your family are doing. She will always be with you guys. When I saw her in my dream, she's a very happy girl."

I wrote back, "Thank you for the kind words, we have two dogs."

She sent another message, "In my dream it was a big brown dog. I don't do this as a profession, but after an accident as a child, I have realized I am clairvoyant, so I try to give these messages to people that come in my dreams."

We had two large chocolate labs. This was the first time I thought, *maybe we don't know everything.* Maybe she is communicating or got a message from Alaina. I could call her crazy or consider that maybe we were afraid of the unknown. Either way, I was curious.

The mysterious events continued. The following year, in the spring of 2019, we were sitting in our living room when a bird flew into the window and crashed against the glass. *Boom.* In the past, usually this killed the bird, and I expected to find its lifeless body on the ground when I went to the front door. I opened it to see a blue bird with light gray wings standing on our porch like he'd come to deliver a package—or just say hello. The bird seemed fine, but I had never seen a bird like it before. Oddly, it also didn't seem to be fazed by my presence on the porch.

The next morning, I woke up to a tapping on my window. When I opened the blinds, the bird was sitting on the top wire of our vineyard adjacent to the bedroom window, staring at me. I went to get dressed and came back to the window to see the bird still sitting there, where it remained for hours in the same spot. I soon began seeing these light blue birds everywhere. If I was sad or depressed but out for a walk or a drive, I would start seeing these birds one after another. I could not deny the sign, and I deeply believe Alaina was sending them.

These events set in motion a series of inquiries that opened me up to the possibility that Alaina was communicating with us. Somehow. Some way. She was sending messages. Through others. Through animals. Even through music. So against everything I believed prior to her death, I reluctantly decided to speak with a medium named Nikki Gross the following January. She was referred by a friend who we knew was a woman of faith. I did not know what to believe when I first made the call, but I was open to anything. My position on faith was evolving. My understanding of life, death, and love had been reborn in our new normal.

What was driving this sudden shift in me? A question pressed on me day after day, night after night. I lay in bed beside my wife wondering how and why an "all-knowing and all-loving" God could allow our daughter and eleven others to be taken in the way they were. It did not make sense to me to think Alaina's murder was a part of His plan. What *was* "His plan"?

This constant battle inside me needed attention because I could not find peace until it ended. What if in my sadness I could communicate with Alaina? I hoped the medium might provide that kind of healing.

I needed to stop this loop. It was not helping me to move on or to let go of what I could never change. It also was not helping me to accept what happened as not only a tragedy, but also an act of God. I know that sounds heretical and I questioned myself for even thinking this, but my journey was leading me to understand God in an entirely different way.

Might the medium help me reframe my understanding of the *way things were?* Could she help me find a way forward and a new kind of logic? I needed to replace the one on which I was desperately relying, but which was failing me day after day. I had so many questions. Do we know everything? Is there really life after death?

What if? What if? *What if?*

I am glad I turned to Nikki. She was extremely gifted and made me feel at ease, instructing me to find a place where I could relax and not be interrupted. *Good luck with that*, I thought, *I can't even find that in my own home at times.* So, I drove up the hill of the Veterans Home of California and backed into a spot overlooking the entrance of the cemetery and some large trees. It felt peaceful there and the right place to make this very odd call to a medium.

I did not expect much but hoped she could help make sense of what was in my head. I was pleasantly surprised that Nikki managed my expectations immediately, saying she was not an evidential medium and explained she would not be telling me there was a red teddy bear or giving me any specifics. She would solely communicate via the messages she received.

Fair enough, right? I appreciated her transparency and was curious to start the session.

Here's what blew my mind. She did not know who I was. She did not research her clients. She met me literally on a cold call after we set up the appointment. I had not told her my story when we began, but the skeptic in me realized she could have looked me up and read about us on social media when she began listing some standard assumptions of Alaina, mentioning a soccer ball and some personality traits. I wasn't that impressed until what she said next. The specificity was so accurate, it was almost spooky, but I knew right then she was the real deal.

I stiffened when she spoke, telling me in real time, "Alaina is telling me her brother, Alex, was around two years of age when he fell while you guys were on vacation. He split his head open. From that time on he had a bit of a black cloud following him and that caused him anxiety." She wasn't asking if it was a question, she was telling me exactly what happened—as if she had seen it herself, just then, as Alaina was relating the story.

Outside my truck where I was taking this call, everything felt super still, but inside my body, it felt like a jet had pushed through the sonic layer in the atmosphere. I heard and felt a *boom*. Only a few people in our world knew about the accident with Alex that had happened many years prior. She was spot on. Our son had been extremely anxious ever since. I was all ears. This was not bullshit. I did not know how she was getting these messages, but the content itself was too specific and accurate to deny what was happening.

What she told me next astounded me.

I listened, without judging this time, while she continued. "Alaina is telling me when she passed, she broke into Horcruxes, like Harry Potter, and gave her confidence to Alex."

Wait a second.

What did she just say?

I didn't move. I took in her words, flashing back to the day we were informed. Alex had no understanding until 6 a.m. that morning that something was wrong. We didn't discuss the what ifs on our way to the airport or on the flight. We approached the Teen Center at Thousand Oaks with as much hope as we could muster and yet with a deep knowing that something awful, something so unspeakable, so unthinkable might have happened to our daughter.

Shortly after, we were all informed, and only a few hours after that, our son, who had bouts of anxiety and worry for most of his childhood, wrote the eulogy for his sister—as if this was standard and usual behavior for a fourteen-year-old kid. When I consider Alex's confidence that night, the words that flowed through him and into his laptop and the absolute grace he possessed when I walked into his hotel room to find him working, I realized that I was looking at another version of our son—his sister showing up through him. Talk about chills.

If the medium was right, and Alaina had somehow transferred her confidence to her brother, then I had no reason to doubt it. Alex has remained strong and confident ever since. He spoke before thousands of people at her funeral as if he'd performed with rock stars or statesmen. He was commanding, cool, calm, open hearted. Just like his sister. There was a new energy about him that nobody could deny or explain—until the medium connected the dots. To top it off, when he applied to college three years later, he chose to study abroad when many students were fearful of attending the local junior college near us during Covid. Alex had set his sights on new horizons, no doubt ushered in by his sister's spirit of unshakable confidence.

Near the end of the session, as if on cue, Nikki announced, "Alaina is telling me you are still skeptical." I had to laugh. There she was again, pushing me to grow. To open. To accept what might be possible, versus looking for the data to believe it was true.

I told Nikki she was right and admitted that I wondered what people would think of me if I told them any of this, but I was desperate to know the truth. Was she a whack job or the real deal? How much more did she need to tell me to convince me that our daughter was right there, probably as we spoke, passing messages to her, to get to me, to wake me up and guide me forward? It's like Alaina was whispering, *Dad, there's another way to see all this. It's not all bad. Just be open minded and look for it, for God's sake!*

She wasn't done communicating either. Of course.

Nikki continued, "Alaina is telling me there is a manilla envelope on a small table, like an end table or a hall table. I am asking her what is on the letter that is in the envelope. She is only smirking. Let me ask her again…No, she is not answering but has this sarcastic smile. I don't know what that means, do you know?"

I replied, "I have no idea." But I did know that smirk. What was she up to? We ended the session with this big question mark, until I got home and found the answer.

A week earlier, I reached out to Detective Chris to see how he was and to thank him again for the helicopter ride.

I had also asked him to send some Sergeant Ron Helus bracelets, honoring the officer who tried to help at Borderline but who was also killed that night. I wanted to give the bracelets to the other three officers who helped us, one for Alfonso and Oscar, who drove Alaina's body home, and one to Deputy Lombardi who ran into the building at the shooting at the Pathway Home in Yountville. Chris agreed to send them to me.

The day of the session with the medium, I arrived home to find a manilla envelope on the hall table below our family portrait which sits between two signs. One says HOPE and the other FAITH. I opened the envelope to see five SGT Ron Helus bracelets. No note. No letter. So when Nikki was asking what is on the letter, she was asking the wrong question. She should have asked what was in the envelope. Thus the sarcastic smile and no response from Alaina.

I would continue to have these God moments as the years progressed after her passing. My mindset has expanded. I am no longer limited by my need for "evidence." The joke was on me. The evidence was all around me, if I could only choose to see it. Eventually, things that used to drive me crazy and feel a bit too "woo-woo" would give me pause. I am no longer as quick to judge or dismiss something that might actually be true, especially if it's out of the ordinary or possibly construed as a bit strange or eccentric. What I realized over time is that what we don't understand fully tends to frighten us. When I turned my compass point to being open to receiving information that was trying to avail itself to me, my life started to change—and often for the better. Things started to take on a magical, holy meaning. I started to see God in the small things, even in the inconveniences or the seemingly annoying detour. I began to live from the mindset of asking myself over and over, "What if it was supposed to go this way after all?" I realized that if I remain open to "let go and let God," I never know what can come of it.

The great thing in my search for meaning, similar to the message on the episode of *God Friended Me*, is that I was beginning to understand that faith was more about my belief that I was making a difference to others. Alaina had previewed what was coming into my life. Now, I could keep looking for it, because maybe she was right. Maybe it was not all bad. Maybe it was also good. Maybe we were beginning to understand things in a fundamentally new way. What if we were blessed with eighteen years of Alaina rather than subject to a lifetime without her?

Imagine

SIX MONTHS AFTER the shooting, I finally managed to look at some posts on Facebook and catch up on the many kind comments friends had left for me over the months. One day in May, I read some posts referring to a TV show called *So You Think You Can Dance*, where a group of kids had choreographed a dance in honor of Borderline 12. I had known about this for a while, but when the show originally aired, I wasn't ready to see it. I was still too raw, too hurting. But by the spring, I finally turned notifications back on and more comments showed up which I could no longer ignore. People were touched. Maybe I was missing something by avoiding this video?

That particular morning in May, I found myself riding another wave of emotions. This time, however, they didn't debilitate me. I reminded myself to breathe and got in my truck, ready to go to work, when the urge struck me to see the dance. I sat there in the driver's seat holding my phone and took a deep breath. I knew if seeing the performance made me even more emotional, I was alone in the privacy of my truck. I searched the posts and found the YouTube link. Part of me hesitated to press play. For so long, Hannah and I did not want to know any details associated with the Borderline shooting. For reasons I've already mentioned, we knew that information would not help us bring our daughter back. If anything, it might cause irrevocable harm —especially if we couldn't free our minds from the savage loop we heard so many others were experiencing. Details would not reverse the finality of death, so we had chosen to avoid any details or even hints of what actually happened that evening. While this might not be the best approach for others, it was and still is the best way for Hannah and me to manage the trauma and not retrigger it. Over the weeks, months, and years, my own mind created pictures of what might have happened, but I always knew they were not real. I was better able to move on and not allow those visions to debilitate me.

 I also knew that this video of a dance was not what happened that night and that it was safe for me to watch. It was a tribute, not a reenactment, and from the comments it seemed that everyone was moved by seeing it. I ran my finger over the steering wheel and finally tapped on the YouTube video. My heart was pounding. Very shortly after pressing play, I watched a number of people doing an interpretive dance that turned chaotic. They were all dressed in black, arms linked. One of the dancers appeared as if they were struck and would start to fall, while the others would lift them back up. This exchange was alternated amongst the dancers, who were embodying what it might look like to be hit by bullets. As the dance came to an end, the performers removed their overshirts on cue and turned around to reveal the word ENOUGH.

The word struck my gut. *ENOUGH.*

The seven letters echoed inside my truck as if they had bounced off the windshield.

I could feel the entire word rip through my body, feet to head, head to feet.

E N O U G H.

I said the word slowly, out loud, and felt my heart pound.

The dancers had borrowed the word, already in use to express how so many were feeling about the shooting—and all the mass shootings we were suffering in our country. The word held significant meaning for me as a huge sports fan and coach. After the shooting, I had heard it used multiple times by NBA players making a public statement about the incident. The LA Clippers and Lakers wore shirts with ENOUGH on the front and the names of the twelve victims on their backs. They had had enough, and it was time for change. I had had enough, and it was time for change. Everyone affected by the shooting had had enough and knew it was time for change. It was time to make a stance against the gun violence in our country. This dance brought it all together in the most unexpected and artistic way. I felt gutted and validated all at once. People were getting it. People were feeling it. Our collective heartache and frustration were finally being seen.

I dropped my phone on the passenger seat, feeling tears roll down my face. I sat there for a few moments before I wiped them, then took a deep breath and told myself it was time to get back to work. I had been trying to get mentally reestablished at my businesses for months. Showing up day after day in a community that knew me, my family, and my story was challenging. There was no place I could be without somebody knowing me. Alaina had also worked the cash register at the store the prior summer. The staff members knew her, so being there was a constant reminder that she was not there. Daily, I was trying to fight the fog and focus. My staff was supportive, knowing that sometimes I was in the building physically but somewhere else mentally. Deep down, it was difficult to focus when so much had changed.

After watching the dance video, I threw my Ford F150 into reverse and started the trek into town. *It was time to focus*, I told myself. *Time to get back to business.* I usually like to listen to music on my way into work and the audio was connected to my phone. Suddenly Beyonce's "Halo" started to play. I had put this song on my playlist for when I ran. I loved the great beat, which helped my rhythm, but I had not been running then. The grief had stolen that need from me, so I had not touched the playlist in months. Even when I had, I never really tuned into the lyrics of this song, but I listened closely this time, as I never had before.

Was Alaina the angel tearing down the walls of our limited ideas of what was possible in this life? Was she trying to tell us day after day that we were capable of not only surviving but using this experience to build an entirely new foundation for our life? Literally and figuratively? Was she everywhere we looked, in the negative space of the sky and the stars, without a body but still with us? I wanted to believe that was true. I wanted to imagine that Alaina was everywhere and always within us. I wanted to believe that this song carried a potent message.

While I sensed Beyonce had someone else in mind when she was writing this song, the lyrics really hit in that moment, especially the chorus. When the song ended, it started again, even though I touched nothing. I felt my heart skip a beat. What was happening? It was all too bizarre. What's even more wild about this is that I *never ever* keep my music on repeat and considered pulling over to get it off repeat while I drove down the frontage road on the west side of Highway 29, passing rows and rows of vineyards—while "Halo" played again.

After it played a second time, I expected it to repeat again, but Halo round three did not begin. Instead, John Lennon's "Imagine" started to play. This was not a song on my running playlist. I had goosebumps. Something was happening. I was touched at the timing of these resounding words in Lennon's song and how appropriate they were for me at that moment.

As I drove past acres of vineyards and the vine trail that Alaina and I ran together several times before she left for college, I suddenly realized the playlist was not mine. It was coming through someone else. I listened to John Lennon's words and felt chills run up my spine. I was being told to imagine there was no heaven. And no hell. I lifted my eyes to the sky wondering if she was there with me at that moment. I considered the possibility that if there was no heaven, and no hell, then was it conceivable that she was still with us—through the music?

As I got closer to my store in Napa, I was thinking, *Okay Alaina, I hear you!* I even said it out loud with a giggle and tears in my eyes.

The music mystery wasn't over. The next two songs were by Brian McKnight. Alaina and I used to sing some of McKnight's songs because she knew I loved R&B. While the lyrics weren't necessarily pertinent, I found myself singing them at the top of my lungs—as if I thought I *could* sing. I didn't care if I was off key. I had no doubt Alaina was singing with me and maybe laughing too. The whole bizarre series of events was one of many inexplicable moments that made me realize I don't understand how she is with us, but I know she will always be with me. This was a seminal moment in my healing. I had truly found my faith. My daughter's presence was apparent. I didn't need anyone to believe me, I was living these moments with her.

Angels from Afar

THE MYSTERIOUS EVENTS had a history. I was not a total stranger to synchronicities. I believed in them. 17 years prior to Alaina's passing, I was already tuning into signs. This time it was with the father of another Alana (with nearly the same spelling) and it began with a terrorist attack on September 11, 2001, when our world changed forever.

We all have our stories of the moment we found out what happened. I was at work when my mom called to tell me a plane struck the Twin Towers. My first response was, "How would someone run into the tower?" and I went back to work. A few minutes later, she called again to share the update about the Pentagon being struck by another plane and informed me the other tower was struck too. I didn't know what to do with the news and felt disoriented in my horror, watching the chaos on TV.

At the same time, Hannah was in San Diego visiting her sister, Theresa, and niece Moorea. Alaina was just a baby and they were supposed to fly home the next day so that Hannah could go back to work at the high school. I called her to discuss our plan.

"They are going to shut down the airports. I don't know if I want you flying anyway, but you won't get home tomorrow, so I am going to drive down to get you both."

Hannah planned to get a ride from her sister and meet me in Corona, California. It was eerie to drive with the airspace free and clear of any planes. On the drive south, I called a friend, Bill, and proposed doing a fundraiser in Yountville for a family affected by 9/11. Bill was a friend who was very involved in the Yountville community and helped organize and support fundraisers. I wanted to do something to help, imagining how it would be for Hannah and Alaina if they had lost me as their husband and father and were struggling to make the mortgage and pay the bills. If there was any way we could reduce the financial burdens for this other family, we would.

Bill was open to the idea and suggested we coordinate with the nonprofits in Napa and throw a big pasta dinner. In the past, we had organized many pasta dinner fundraising events for the elementary school and knew we could do this quickly. Bill agreed, which made me feel good on the long drive down to Corona to pick up Hannah and Alaina.

Hannah was equally excited about doing the pasta dinner, having no idea how it would all circle back, seventeen years later.

We stayed the night in Corona and drove home the next day, listening to updates on the radio, struck by the chaos and sadness. When we got back, we met with Bill and planned the fundraising dinner near Halloween—an all-you-can-eat pasta dinner for $10 per person. Although we had no additional auction, participants could make an additional donation for a glass of wine or a beer. We hollowed out a huge pumpkin and encouraged people to fill it with as much or as little money as they could.

At that time, we still didn't have a beneficiary. We just knew that we wanted to help one family in need. We met with the nonprofit leaders and discussed the Red Cross or fire fighters and other first responder foundations, which all felt like good options. Prior to the meeting, I was doing something that many hadn't done—conduct a search on the "World Wide Web." Crazy, right? At the time, it was. Most people weren't turning to their computers like this to find what I was looking for—a family we could help. I searched the obituaries in the *New York Times*, which proved challenging even though it sounds like a simple task. It was a lot harder to do this in September 2001, especially on a dial-up internet service. I finally found a list of every person who had died, including families requesting donations to the organizations mentioned previously. I finally found a family seeking help:

McGOVERN-*Scott Martin. Age 35 of Wyckoff, NJ. Victim of World Trade Center Disaster, September 11, 2001. Cherished husband of Jill (nee Shaffro). Adored father of Alana and Nicole.*

Loving son of Elisabeth Scott and Martin McGovern, stepson of Anne McGovern. Beloved son-in-law to Renee and William Shaffro. Devoted brother to Tara, brother-in-law to Raymond, Ronni and Steven. Memorial Service Friday, September 28, 2001, 1 p.m. at Christ Church, Franklin Avenue and Cottage Place, Ridgewood, New Jersey. In lieu of flowers, contributions to the Scott McGovern Family Fund would be appreciated.

This was the only name I found asking for a contribution to a family fund and his oldest daughter was Alana. Not quite the same as Alaina, yet close enough for me. It felt right.

I contacted Sharon, the owner of the local Yountville Sun newspaper and asked her to make sure it wasn't a scam. She contacted a family friend of the McGovern family and confirmed the story. Sharon also found the following story that had been published only a week before by the *Trenton Times* on September 25, 2001.

On Christmas morning 1989, a struggling waitress and single mother living in a dreary basement flat in Staten Island woke up to find a set of Matchbox cars and a snowsuit on the doorstep for her son, accompanied only by a card that said: "To Eric. Love, Santa." The woman, Susan Trainor, did not know who had left the presents.

Then, in September 2001, Susan Trainor picked up a newspaper and saw a memorial notice for an old friend, Scott McGovern, written by his mother. "He had his silent charities," Ms. Trainor said she read from the notice. "He knew a woman with a toddler, and on Christmas Eve..." Ms. Trainor stopped reading and began to cry.

That was Scott M. McGovern to a T, said his wife, Jill McGovern. Mr. McGovern, 35, a trader at Euro Brokers in 2 World Trade Center, was always trying to figure out how to make someone happy. Just before bedtime, Ms. McGovern said, her husband would pick up Alana, the older of their two daughters, wrap her in a blanket and walk out to the driveway of their house in Wyckoff, NJ. "Where are you going?" Ms. McGovern would ask them. Scott would whisper back, "We're going to wish on a star."

I stopped reading and knew the McGovern Family would be our beneficiary. I showed the obituary to Bill and the others, and after Sharon confirmed the story, we were off. By the end of October 2001, we sent the McGovern Family Foundation a check for more than $8,000.

Shortly after, I received a phone call from Jill McGovern. We were both in tears.

"Why did you do this?" she asked.

"Because if it were to happen to me, I would want someone to step up and help Hannah and Alaina." We had a wonderful conversation and she told me some stories about Scott. While I never knew him, I felt like we shared a connection in some way.

Fast forward 17 years. We'd remained in contact with Jill, and not long after the news of the shooting, I got a message from her in Wyckoff, NJ. The town was told about our story and how we were connected to Wyckoff in our actions of kindness toward the McGovern family after 9/11. The community across the country raised money to have an olive tree dedicated on the Pepperdine campus. Alaina's tree dedication was beautiful and so meaningful. Her suitemates and many others painted rocks and placed them around the tree. It was such a beautiful gesture; we could never thank Jill and the Wyckoff community enough for their kindness. They also had another gesture in the making. They contracted with the nonprofit Splashes of Hope to paint a mural to be installed at a children's hospital of our choosing. One had become available in Oakland, California. Not only did we get to choose this hospital, but Splashes of Hope also invited the families to help paint parts of the mural —as a way to heal. The murals would add cheer to the hospital wards and were always dedicated to someone. Splashes of Hope offered everyone involved with a mural the chance to take part in their healing.

This was an astonishing part of our grieving process. Nearly a year after the shooting, we were invited by our dear friends at Black Stallion Winery, along with extended family, friends, and many other people who loved us, to help paint parts of the mural. It was an unbelievably healing event in September 2019. In the midst of feeling powerless over our tragedy, we realized we always had choices in how we responded to it. We could sit back in our grief and bewilderment and do nothing, or we could find a way to help another person in their own pain and suffering. This choice was hardwired in me and the key to moving forward after losing Alaina. While we were sadly connected to Jill McGovern because we both endured unimaginable tragedy, we also found hope, love, kindness and light after our darkest days.

We had been angels from afar to Jill, inspired by her husband Scott's acts of kindness. Our lives are forever altered by his legacy of "wishing upon a star" with his daughter. It just takes one small gesture to make a difference, and that difference can uplift an entire community. If there was ever doubt about angels in our midst, I never doubted them from that moment on because any of us can be that angel for another human being.

A week after the mural painting, our dear friend Megan, who organized Alaina's church memorial, joined us to paint a mural with her family. I have a picture of her daughter, Addie, painting with us. She was six years old, showing up to join in her community and give back as her family modeled. My stomach dropped when I received a group message from the local soccer organization that I had worked with for a decade: *Guys, there has been an accident and one of our soccer players has passed away. We are keeping it under wraps for now, but we might need to do something fast to support. Will keep you in the loop.*

I reached out to the person who sent the message in the event that Hannah and I could offer immediate support. He told me it was Addie, Megan's daughter. My heart pounded and I felt sick. Apparently, a stack of catering chairs accidentally fell and crushed her when they were setting up for a family event. I could not believe the devastating news. She was six years old. I thought I was going to throw up. She had been at our house only one week prior.

I immediately called Hannah. We were so sad, recounting this little girl eating dinner with us and having a great time contributing to the mural. The thought of any family going through such heartache was unfathomable to us, even though we had lost our own daughter. Alaina was 18. Addie was six. Death doesn't discriminate and doesn't care about age or timing. But we did. I closed my eyes and prayed that Alaina was there to meet and comfort Addie in her passing.

I contacted a cousin of the family and offered to help. "Please let us know if we can help or come over to be with Megan and Jason. At the same time, we don't expect to be needed, just know we are here."

The response, "Yes please, they'd love to see you guys."

Addie's family was ready and willing to receive help and support. Hannah and I were glad for their choice. Seeing another family go through this apparent post-traumatic growth process, after extreme tragedy, really resonated with us. Instead of dwelling on what they had lost, they chose to celebrate the life that they knew and loved and still do to this day. Although they were still processing extreme sorrow and grief, they chose to be surrounded by so much love. The family decided to recognize Addie's love with the phrase: "Live Rad."

In our small community, the support was expanding exponentially, and the band of angels was present in full force. It was a radical way to dance with grief and turn all our pain into love. One day, years later, I would stumble upon the poem, "Everything is Waiting for You," by David Whyte. It spoke to me of the inverse ratio between the depth of our grief and the depth of our love.

Despite the tendency to believe the opposite, often in our darkest moments, the world is reaching out to us to remind us that we are not alone.

Calling from the Heavens

I NEEDED TO remember this kind of synchronicity during the agonizing nights that followed Alaina's murder. For nearly a year after the shooting, I was waking up around 12:36 in the morning, almost every day—the time that we got the call. I didn't know why I kept doing this but have since realized that I was in a trauma loop. My body was being retriggered around the same time when all this went down. It was a recurring alarm from hell that I couldn't turn off. I had no idea that I had hopped on the PTSD merry-go-round—obviously, minus the merry.

During this phase of my grief and healing, more coincidences related to Alaina's passions and presence in our lives continued. Often, I found myself seeing words or thinking of phrases but I didn't know why. They were not my words or thoughts, and most were related to songs or lyrics. Music, it seemed, would be Alaina's greatest way to stay connected with us.

Although I enjoyed learning music when I was young, I did not pursue it like my daughter. Alaina, on the other hand, had found her voice in music early on. Given her Filipino heritage, she was naturally supposed to take piano lessons. Hannah and I joked about when she would start. Everyone in Hannah's family took piano lessons, so it was no surprise when Alaina, at the age of four, told us she wanted to play the piano too.

She studied for about seven years, but it was always a chore with the traditional way of teaching music. During those years, she learned recorder at school and violin, which she played for about five years through early high school. Alex tried guitar and lasted about five lessons. Soccer was his passion, so the guitar found its way into Alaina's room, as did a ukulele she wanted to get when we were in Hawaii. She studied both and loved playing around with the instruments, but she wasn't huge into performing for others. Alaina said she had stage fright, yet she would always be singing, humming, and grooving to the music around the house.

One day during her junior year, she surprised us when she told us she entered the Junior Miss competition—a college scholarship program for high school seniors that involved a talent competition. This was a bit of a surprise for her mom and me, yet we loved that she was trying it. Her talent in the competition was to play the ukulele and sing "Fools Rush In." It brought us tears of pride seeing her stand and nail that song both on instrument and her voice. It was her first time before an audience on the stage and she appeared so at ease. She was beaming with joy, sharing her gifts with not only us but people she had never met. She had discovered something about herself in that competition—which would oddly resurface *after* the shooting.

One year after Borderline, I was starting to hear lyrics. This was a complete one-off for me. Remember, I never thought I had a creative bone in my body, but the words were coming and I knew they were a song. While I wasn't exactly certain Alaina was responsible for this, I knew I needed to ask a musically minded person what to do with them. I reached out to my friend Elliot, whom I had known from Napa Valley and who had also been a *Sigma Chi* Fraternity brother from Pepperdine. We met up on a beautiful sunny day in Yountville at Southside Café, where Elliot was waiting with his girlfriend Holly, known in the music industry as Skylar Gray. She is not only a very talented musician but also a wonderful person. I was a little nervous to tell them why I had asked them to meet but managed to blurt it out when we were seated at the table.

"I don't know why but lyrics are in my head," I said, "I've got lots of words coming to me, but I don't know how to put them together and thought I would ask for your help."

Two weeks later, Elliot and Holly called. "Arik, we need you to hear something." The excitement made me curious. They sent me a song called "Calling from the Heavens."

The title alone gave me chills and I took a deep breath.

Holly explained, "Arik, I didn't know Alaina and it wasn't something I was prepared to take on, but this morning I woke up to the sound of an alarm and I started writing."

Holly explained that she had never written a song in the third person but found herself writing madly all morning while the words flooded her. At lunch, it dawned on Elliot what was happening, "Holly, you know you're writing this for Alaina?"

Holly sounded awed by the experience. "And that was when I realized what it was. When it's complete in the next couple of days, I will send it over. I hope you like it."

When I hung up, I lifted my eyes and shook my head. Alaina was at it again, staying connected to us through the music. Hannah and I were deeply touched by the whole gesture. When we had the chance to listen for the first time, we were struck by the similarity in voice in a harmony piece that sounded as if it could be Alaina singing in the tone and pitch.

Calling from the Heavens

Never knew a smile was such a fragile thing
Only takes a moment for it all to change
She was calling on the phone just yesterday
But she's calling from the heavens now,
calling from the heavens now

Sending down a kiss in every drop of rain
I see her in the mirror there inside my face
I swear I hear her singing when the music plays
She's calling from the heavens now,
calling from the heavens and

She's falling like the rain
She's falling like the rain
Falling like the rain

She's calling from the heavens now,
calling from the heavens now
She has always been my angel's face
I hope I meet her in the sky one day
Until then all I can do is pray
And call up to the heavens,
call up to the heavens and

She's falling like the rain
Falling like the rain
Falling like the rain

She's calling from the heavens now,
calling from the heavens now
Never knew a smile was such a fragile thing
Only takes a moment for a heart to break
She was calling on the phone just yesterday
But she's calling from the heavens now,
calling from the heavens now

Calling from the heavens now
Calling from the heavens now
Calling from the heavens now
Calling form the heavens now
Calling from the heavens now
Calling from the heavens now

Calling from the heavens now
Calling from the heavens and

She's falling like the rain
She's falling like the rain
Falling like the rain
Falling like the rain
She's falling like the rain

She was calling on the phone just yesterday
But she's calling from the heavens now,
calling from the heavens now

Hannah was moved to tears hearing the song for the first time. She turned to me in awe and asked, "How did she know?"

"What?" I asked.

"It was like she read my mind. Some of those exact words were in my head!" she said.

We hugged and cried, so moved by the love, and at how hard the words hit home.

A New Hard

IN APRIL 2022, when Alaina would have graduated from Pepperdine, the school asked if we would like Alaina's name announced with her graduating class. It was a kind and thoughtful gesture offered by some students. Hannah and I discussed it and concluded she was not meant to be there yet appreciated the opportunity. Instead, we suggested the students could decide if they wanted a moment of silence to recognize Alaina and another student who had recently passed from their class. But there was no way we could go to Pepperdine this time. Watching her suitemates walk the stage would have been too hard, and we were committed to living in the present for our son. Alex was a senior and had plenty of soccer games and other activities. We didn't need to be reminded that Alaina would not walk the stage on graduation day or any day.

However, Hannah and I made our way to some graduation parties for Alaina's best friend Maria. The two were inseparable for years and both shared a love for musicals. I remember like it was last week when they finally decided to watch *West Side Story*. While they were watching from the living room couch, I walked past them and recalled the lines to the movie I'd watched in high school. I snapped my fingers and sang, "When you're a jet, you're a jet all the way. From your first day in class till your last dying day." Then I quickly walked out of the room and ran back through, leaping and yelling "POW!" like the fight scene. The girls thought it was hysterical. They were doubled over laughing at me and with me. My memories of these two girls almost always conjure up our living room, the couch, the television, and their huge smiles.

Maria was like family to us, so we were determined to go to her graduation party. We approached her home tucked into the rolling landscape of the Coombsville area in east Napa. As we drove up, I realized my family lived in the house next door when I was born. Emotions started flooding me on what would have been a milestone day for our daughter. Everything was coming full circle. I felt overwhelmed by it all. I looked at Hannah and we took a deep breath. I grabbed her hand, and we managed to walk into the backyard graduation party.

This was not going to be easy. While it was nice to see some of her classmates and their parents, the awkwardness was palpable. Understandably. Our daughter was not there with us or her friends. We shared stories and small talk, yet I could tell a few were holding back in conversation, unsure how comfortable the moment was, for us. When it came time to leave, I was really struggling to hold back my emotions. Alaina would never have a graduation party. This was the first kind of major milestone where we felt her absence that no lyrics could fill.

Four months later, in the fall of 2022, I stopped by our friends' Dave and Lorrie's house. Their oldest niece Julia was getting married the next day and we were invited. As usual Dave was doing what he does, yard work, without complaint. At least not to me. He was all sweaty, mowing the front lawn of their Stags Leap district front landscape, a terraced rock wall with a lush lawn and breathtaking view of vineyards up the hillside and across the entire swath of Yountville appellation to the eastern facing hills of Oakville. It was stunning.

I was stopping to see if they needed any help in the preparation. Ironically, a new beer had arrived that day at my grocery store called Wedding Day by Henhouse and I thought it would be funny to drop some cold cans by and say hello. Daved stopped the lawn mower and I handed him a can of "Wedding Day." Just then, a golf cart rolled up to us with his brother Ernie and sister-in-law Ginette, they were the father and mother of the bride-to-be, and another friend of theirs was in the back seat.

All of us stood on the lawn drinking Wedding Day, enjoying a few hallmark smartass comments. I thought nothing of this exchange. We were so happy for his family and for Julia, the young bride.

The next day, we attended the wedding with my parents, only five miles from our home. Due to a lack of parking and the alcohol we knew we would consume, we agreed to have my parents pick us up so that we could help them with the walking part and assist my mom after her many surgeries. But nobody said anything about "the obvious." We were headed to a wedding of a twenty-something woman, but Alaina's absence was present, suspended between our words and our thoughts. This is the invisible rope strung between those who have lost loved ones. And while we didn't think we had brought her absence with us, it connected us in our pain.

After years of Covid, seeing the wedding site and everyone so dressed up was very special. It was refreshing to see people together, happy, and connecting. We were so excited for Julia and her soon-to-be husband, Tucker. They had shared their first kiss at our house at one of our annual New Year's parties long ago, and I don't remember who was more excited, the kids, her mom Ginette or her Auntie Lorrie.

When it came time to sit down for the wedding, everything felt perfect. My parents wanted us to sit with them, but we waited to make sure everyone else got a seat first. The truth was I sensed this was going to be a bit emotional for me, and I needed a bit of space. I preferred to be in the back just in case it was all too much and I needed to get out and be alone to reground.

As the music began, Hannah and I took a seat in the last section of chairs. We waited there a few minutes in anticipation with everyone else. Finally, I saw Ernie and Ginette walking their daughter down the aisle. Julia was radiant, beaming, in love, with her future in front of her. And it hit. The force of emotion struck like a tsunami. I'd had a feeling it might—but hoped to be hidden and in the privacy of my wife when it did. My throat tightened and I was holding back the tears as much as possible, not for embarrassment, but to avoid making others feel pity for us, which I neither wanted nor needed. It was one of many moments that we realized would continue in our life-long journey with this grief.

Because here was the gut-wrenching truth. Alaina would never walk down the aisle, and Hannah and I would never get to do that for and with her. The pain of this was practically unbearable. I reminded myself to breathe. I sat there taking in the enormity of the joy and despair dancing side by side in that moment. This duality of grief struck me hard.

There would be many more moments like this, small, subtle, quiet moments where the grief would rise up and wallop me over the years, but eventually, I found a way to accept what is—even while I was swallowing the millionth lump in my throat. I would find a way to accept that the pain would come but also go. There was a wild wave cycle to all of this if I just allowed for it to happen and didn't try to suppress it or distract myself from the universal laws of grief. Trying to fight it would be like fighting gravity and I did not have that kind of energy to waste.

I was learning that recovery from loss is not measured by not feeling the pain anymore, but by how we have been able to alchemize the pain into some other energy that helps us move forward. I knew I needed to move forward after that wedding. I would never move on, but I would move forward with a deep hole. That is grief, I have learned. The hole that resides inside us, the emptiness that exists and never seems to be filled, but which becomes more bearable, day after day. All these moments would be painful, but they would be our new normal.

The following year on a cold Sunday night in February, I found myself wanting to get home and plop on the couch after being at the soccer field. It was an unusually wet winter, and for the first time since I was a kid, I saw snow on the surrounding mountains. Perhaps it was a sign that anything was possible. When I entered our living room, I saw Hannah sitting on the couch, watching a show. We greeted each other as if everything was normal, but as I approached, I saw tears welling in her eyes.

I quietly asked her, "Were you crying, love?"

She gave a slight smile and looked at the TV. "*Mulan* was just on."

I turned to see the closing credits rolling behind me.

She continued, "It was the last scene when the daughter was reunited with the parents."

I turned and looked into her eyes and we both started tearing up. We did not have to say anything else. There was an amazing amount of nonverbal communication that happened between Hannah, Alex, and me. In this instance, the reuniting with the daughter struck a chord. I had come to know that sometimes just a lyric or some image would retrigger our grief, but rather than dwell in the pain, I chose to remind myself that these moments were equally about love too.

A week later, Hannah and I were cleaning the kitchen and putting dishes into our cabinets. We began speaking about messages and moments like this and Hannah said, "Oh I wish I could hold her again or just be with her again." I said, "I wish so much." We paused and held each other, feeling all the emotions stirred up once again, accepting the new and the hard, knowing that there would be lighter times, brighter times, but it was up to us to create them.

Thankfully, laughter has held our family together throughout most of our lives, especially on Hannah's side of the family where the Filipino culture exudes a welcome levity. In October 2023, we gathered in Colorado for the wedding of one of Alaina and Alex's cousins, Sarah.

Two nights before the wedding, the engaged couple were on their way to our Airbnb to pick up some decorations that Grandma had ordered for them off "The Amazon," as she liked to say in her Filipino accent. When we opened up one of the packages and pulled out a sign with loose hanging letters, Hannah read "SAM-E-PENIS." Then someone realized Grandma had bought a sign that said SAME PENIS. To hang on the wall. We didn't expect that from Grandma, yet the house erupted in laughter. It became even funnier when the second sign said: FOREVER.

As the wedding day approached, I found myself eager to stay busy. I could feel the angst building in me, and while I said nothing to Hannah, we both felt this growing sense of dread. While I helped to set up and decorate as best as I could, the moment I saw Sarah's parents walk her down the aisle, the happiness and sadness slammed me simultaneously. The paradox was there again. Hannah and I squeezed each other's hands, doing everything we could to be present. It was a beautiful ceremony, and we wanted to experience the joy for our niece.

During the reception, we found a fireplace in one corner of the room. The mantle was decorated in memory of those who could not attend the wedding. When I saw Alaina's beautiful face and beaming smile among the photos, I paused to take in a breath, struck by the kindness of this gesture to honor these family members. Nobody had told us, and the discovery was so powerful in our privacy. The emotions were running very high for me, and I excused myself to use the bathroom. When I returned, it was the start of the father-daughter dance. I quietly walked through the back of the room while my brother-in-law Matt was dancing with his daughter. As I crossed the room, it seemed as if Alaina's photo was looking straight at me. My heart pounded and I slid out the door near the bar for some fresh air. Not long after, Hannah joined me. She asked if I was alright and gave me a long hug. We held each other in tears for a couple of minutes, reminded once again. The grief would come and go. Unannounced. Unexpected. Yet omnipresent. We might heal but would still feel the pain of our loss for years.

Beach Ball of Grief

AS I REFLECT on the years leading up to Alaina's murder, our family was being prepared in the strangest of ways to cope with the unthinkable. Whenever people ask me, "How were you able to function after such an unthinkable tragedy?" I say, "To be honest, you will be surprised what you can handle. I know I was." I am not a magician. Or a miracle worker. I am not special. But I know that whatever kind of hard heads your way, it is possible to survive what you never thought was possible, especially if you open yourself and allow others to love and support you.

One year before Alaina's murder, in November 2017, I was sitting in St. John's Church in Napa during a Catholic mass with some friends. I was having trouble focusing. When I woke up that day, things felt off, so I wasn't surprised that it was hard to sit in church. My mind tended to drift a bit so my inability to focus wasn't alarming, but soon my phone began to buzz. It was hard to ignore, but I didn't want to check messages during the service, so I turned it off.

After the mass, some friends with us said they received a notice that there was an accident involving the Horn family—friends who had been a vital part of the Napa sports community. This explained why my phone was buzzing and why I woke up feeling "off." As much as I believed I wasn't tuned into events like this, my body was aware something had happened.

A drunk driver hit the Horn family on Interstate 80. Jared Horn, the oldest son, who was driving, was the only survivor. Daryl, his son Joe, his brother, and his nephew all passed. My heart sank. Only three weeks prior, Daryl Horn and I had a conversation in the parking lot of my store. We had been friends through coaching, and I admired his humor and kindness on the field. We bonded early as Chelsea FC fans, too, and had recently spoken about the possibility of starting a wooden bat summer baseball league in Napa. Daryl was the kind of guy who got things done; he was a salesman by trade but a coach by passion, and I absolutely revered him. He nicknamed every kid and was super positive with them on the field. When other coaches would scream at sub-par players, Daryl would shout out words of encouragement like Ted Lasso, "Great job, B-dog, there is no way you could've seen that play. Just keep going!" In instances like this, the kid would run up to him and give him a high-five—in the middle of a game. Daryl would look at us calmly—the other team—and we'd try hard not to pee ourselves laughing.

He was so good with those kids and had a great sense of humor. One year when Alex was in Little League, we had scheduled our teams to play each other on Mother's Day. I was worried this might upset the moms and turned to him for advice.

"Daryl, what should we do for our game next week? It's Mother's Day!"

He flashed his big Daryl grin and winked.

"Don't worry. It's easy!"

I stared at him, wondering what he was thinking.

"Easy?!" I asked, alarmed. "Do you understand American Mother's Day?"

He laughed. "Maybe not but I understand moms! We get some roses and before the game, all the kids run out and give their moms a rose. And all is well. Works every time."

Roses. For the moms. Simple. Easy.

I remember thinking this guy is a fucking genius.

When the game day rolled around, I realized, "Oh shit, I forgot the roses!"

I turned to a friend and a great dad, Steve, whose son was on my team.

"Steve, go to the store and get some roses for the kids to give to the moms for Mother's Day."

Steve looked at me startled.

"Great idea! It's Mother's Day! The moms will love it!"

We both shrugged. Men. We forget these things. But moms don't. Steve had my back and every other dad's back that day. We'd get everyone off the hook thanks to Daryl Horn's Mother's Day Miracle. We had twelve kids on the team. It was a simple mission. Get a dozen roses. Steve took off and I don't know if he went to the store himself, or sent his wife, because he returned with three times what we needed. I figured no problem.

I walked across the field and told Daryl, " I got the roses. How do you want to do it?" Now Daryl looked alarmed. "Oh shit, I forgot to get some!" We shared a chuckle.

He stared at me, panicked. I couldn't believe it. Calm, cool Daryl Horn looked a bit undone. I thought, *Well I can't have my kids do that and not his.*

"Don't worry, Steve got enough for the entire league."

We both laughed but I swear I caught Daryl flick some sweat off his brow. We split the roses between our teams. Everyone had plenty and the presentation went over well. The moms were touched. The players were pumped. And the game was great.

Daryl was my friend, and I could not imagine coaching without him in our league. The news struck hard. Not long after, we were at a candlelight vigil in front of the Horns' house, when I remember trying to stuff my grief inside an invisible closet.

I didn't want Hannah, Alaina, or Alex to see me cry. Every message I had ever received about moments like these had informed me to "be strong." I was a man, right? I was not to express my emotions. As a father, I had to be the rock for my family. Chin up. Carry on. This too shall pass. I did everything I could to shift that grief around, but it was growing heavier by the minute—especially as long as I tried to repress it. Grief, I would learn, doesn't like to be stuffed into a closet—or anywhere really. Grief was knocking on my door telling me it might have been an unwanted guest, but it had a right to be there.

    I ignored the bastard—until the first tear was shed. I tried to hide it and wiped my face so nobody would see me, but to no avail. The gig was up. I stood among our friends on the street in front of their home with candles flickering, seeing flowers—and roses. I could not believe a drunk driver had stolen Daryl from us and taken his youngest son, as well as his brother-in-law and nephew. There was no way to understand any of this.

    I was torn between anger and despair. How would his family survive all this? What could we do now? Who would be there to cheer on the players and give everyone a nickname? I not only lost the guy who epitomized the kind of coach I wanted to be, I had lost a brother in spirit. I choked back a sob but wanted to wail. It hurt so damn much. The harder I tried to conceal it, the worse it became.

    I overheard Alaina ask Hannah, "Why is dad crying?"

    I looked over at her and said, "He was my friend."

    What I really wanted to say but couldn't find the words then was how bewildered I was to see his wife Denise, daughter Greta, and son Jared standing there, when the rest of their family had died. How were they standing in front of people with such poise, in this moment? Little did I know, that would be me. And my wife. And my son. Surviving Alaina. And there would be someone, just like I was at the Horns' service, wondering how do we do it too? How could we go on and live?

That is the mystery of the human spirit. Somehow, I was learning, we all *do* survive.

I began to wonder why people come into our lives—only to lose them too early. For the next twelve months, an odd awareness started to grow inside me about the ephemeral nature of things. I was not a Buddhist, but certain Zen-like understandings casually floated around me, ironically as I continued to stifle my grief. I went back to work and recalled the last conversation with Daryl Horn in my parking lot, wondering why the hell it had to go like this. All the while, I would muscle my way out of feeling the grief which by then had grown so huge that my closet could no longer contain it.

Just like the weeks after the Horn family death, the bewilderment after losing Alaina seemed to be growing exponentially as the shock of the trauma continued. Experts in trauma will tell you that there is a ninety-day period after bad things happen when everyone is adjusting to what they call psychological immunity. Many say nobody is immune from feeling the heavy, the dark, the slow-moving days where despair, disbelief and depression dance. For me, there was seemingly immediate acceptance and sorrow. I wasn't in denial and didn't have anger, but fuck was I sad at times—and still am! Usually after that ninety-day period, two pathways appear: One is a continuation of PTSD, the other branches off to PTG—post-traumatic growth—which has emerged from 15 years of clinical studies and research. It turns out that people either stay stuck in their trauma or apply a growth mindset and heal completely.

I wanted to heal. Hannah wanted to heal. Alex, by his unique response, was already healing because perhaps he saw no other choice. There was an entire life to be lived. He wasn't going to choose to stay stuck anywhere. He was growing up faster than we could have ever believed possible. But his mom and dad? We were a little slower in our efforts to heal completely, not because we didn't want to, but because we had lived for so long without ever going through a tragedy like this. We needed time to adjust, and we needed patience to do that. When we first got home after the shooting, we met with our friend John, who was a therapist. He could not take us on for obvious reasons but sat down with us to discuss some other therapists he suggested. Hannah and I met with him for an hour to understand some of the basics we were going through and to state where we were individually. I'll never forget what he told us.

"Grief is like a beach ball, it's not heavy but there is an emptiness."

Yes, I thought. *Exactly.*

I thought about this a million times since and considered the buoyancy of a beach ball. I can try my best to keep it submerged under water, so no one sees my beach ball of grief, but at some point, life can come in waves and will push me off balance just enough that the ball I was hiding unexpectedly pops up out of the water once again—and shows to those around me. Believe me, I know how the mechanism works. That day at the Horn family memorial, I was there in my private pool of loss, trying my hardest to hold my beach ball underwater. I needed to be strong and stoic. I was sitting on that thing... until I wasn't. Who's the guy who brought his colorful beach ball to the vigil? Not me. I worked hard to keep it still, hidden beneath the surface. The harder I try to keep that ball underwater, out of sight, the more effort and energy it consumes. In hindsight, no one was judging me for my emotions in such a tragic setting and if they were, fuck them, he was my friend.

That's what grief feels like.

Try as we might, it's hard to hold a beach ball under the water.

It takes inordinate energy to suppress our grief. But here's the truth I've learned over the years. If I try to hide my grief from others and myself, I expend tremendous effort pushing my beach ball under the water. But no matter how much time passes, that beach ball is still there. And so is my effort in trying to contain it because all it takes is something small to get me off balance and there is that damn beach ball popping up again, months, years, or decades later. I will carry that beach ball with me for the rest of my life. While I might be able to hide it from time to time by pushing it under the water, it takes a lot more strength and energy to push it under water than to hold it up and carry it. The key is learning how to carry grief without it having power over us.

Let's face it. That is easier said than done. Grief is very much like a toddler. It likes its tantrums, in private, for the most part, but in public too. Ever know those people who the *Tao of Pooh* refers to as "Eeyores"? The guy who bemoans everything because life stole his joy? You name it, he's never happy. He has to blame everyone and everything for his unhappiness when it was his own choice in letting grief control him. In some instances, this need to continue grieving is some people's only connection to the person they have lost—which I totally get, but they combine their sadness with an unwillingness to let go, move on with their loss, and live with gratitude for still having their life. It's not easy to do when someone shoots your child. Trust me. I know I could have chosen to suffer for the rest of my life. But I know my daughter wouldn't allow those antics. Alaina would have pointed her finger from the heavens and frowned, wondering why I was not doing what she would have wanted—for me to live. To laugh. To find my way back to joy. I was her father. Maybe the only choice I had was to show her, even in death, how to keep living. I don't know. It's just a theory.

But here's what I began to notice from the others around me who were also carrying their beach ball of grief in a way that informed me there was another way to hold it. People who are intimate with their own grief also emanate an inner confidence not found in those unfamiliar with deep despair and loss. For all of us who have lost, we recognize the beach ball we each carry. I see how much my parents carry theirs. Individually and as a couple. They hurt so much. My dad is a big guy, born in the mid-forties. He's a business owner and an only child. He's always done things his way. The thought of losing his granddaughter was not in the plan. He and my mom love so deeply, and they also hurt so deeply as they were not able to be there to save Alaina. My mom and dad are also from a generation that thinks if you go to a therapist, you are considered crazy. They wonder why a therapist should tell them how to feel. Ironically, they don't understand that it is not the job of a therapist to manage your feelings—or change them in any way—but to help you understand why you are feeling what you're feeling. I can't believe that I had to learn that going to therapy doesn't make you weak or crazy so that I could inform them as well. Their generation is not as open as mine in seeking this kind of support. It wasn't anything they could have ever prepared for—or foreseen. They have so much love for their family and this tragedy was unfathomable to them and still is. It is much easier for them to push their beach ball of grief under the water and pretend it's not there in public.

If you're grieving now, know that you have options for how you handle your beach ball. I can tell you that allowing others to see you carry it with the kind of quiet resolve I had seen in others who refused to allow the grief to control them ended up living much fuller, enriched lives, despite the degree of loss. I would hope that people would find a way to some kind of supportive therapy—not because anything is wrong with them for seeking it in the first place, but because grief is a part of being human. It is okay not to feel happy all the time. It is okay to say you're not okay and in the exact same moment feel grateful for being alive. The Sufi mystics define a *dervish* as one who stands on the threshold of deep transformation. Grief is the door. If you choose to open it, it will take you through exponential growth—and yet it will not remove the loss or the residual pain. It will just allow you to live without it governing your life.

After losing Alaina, I will carry that beach ball for the rest of my days. Yet now I know it is my choice in how I respond to it. I can try to sit on it, push it down, hide it in my closet, or find some way to make it lighter and bat it over the heads of those at the great concert we call our life. Not everyone is given such a beach ball, and not everyone will feel, at times, destroyed by it. But the beach ball remakes us. It puts us back together, not always better, but more capable of handling whatever life wants us to experience next. I would not trade a minute of my time with Alaina; I just wish I didn't get my beach ball for her so young. It would take the unthinkable to teach me that some people, including my own daughter, come into our lives for a moment and that is enough for them to occupy a place in our hearts forever—right beside the grief. Finding a way to allow these to coexist would become a lifelong practice for me and Hannah.

Part Two

THE THINKABLE

New Relationships

TO MANY PEOPLE, losing a child in a mass shooting is only unthinkable. End of conversation. For me and my family, we had to find another way to travel the grief journey. We found it by following the grooves of a new trail—referred to by counselors, therapists, and researchers as post-traumatic growth (PTG). And let's face it. Admission was not without paying the piper in our collective grief. No doubt, we had been basting in PTSD long enough, but we knew we had agency in how our lives would unfold after the grief became the new normal. Little did we know the trail of PTG would offer unexpected delights, new opportunities, new friendships—grace. While grief is unavoidable, much like gravity, grace is unexpected but available to anyone who is open enough to receive it. We were ready. And what I am about to share in the second part of this book is the unimaginable beauty and love that grew in the place of Alaina's absence.

At first, I had never heard of PTG, but after a friend introduced the concept, the lights went on and have stayed on ever since. Given the darkness we had survived, we welcomed light. Lots of it. PTG would light up the path and give us hope, humor, and infinite support while we rebuilt our lives and reset our compass. Our true north: restore ourselves, and if possible, renew a sense of hope, purpose, and joy to the days that we would live without our daughter living too. It is not easy to take this path, but it was there, and while we had no idea that our initial choices reflected the five aspects of post-traumatic growth, they make complete sense to us now.

One unexpected yet often welcome outcome of trauma is a change in current relationships, and also the opportunity to form new ones. Hannah and I had always been blessed by a strong network of friends, which helped us navigate the earliest days of our devastation. However, we never expected nor could foresee how our world would *expand* because of the other people who would appear to us, linked with our trauma.

I don't know if this was God's way of bestowing a booby prize on the worst thing a parent could survive, but I know my wife and I graciously received this bizarre and blessed phenomenon. It's almost as though there were universal laws of grief that we were slowly beginning to understand over the years after Alaina's death. We felt blessed by the relationships we shared in connection with the families of other victims of Borderline and those assigned to help us navigate our stark new reality. One of those people was a great man, Deputy Chris, who was assigned as our liaison and served as a point of contact if we had any questions regarding the shooting or any related investigations.

It was easy to become quick friends with Chris, who had also lost his good friend and former partner, Sgt. Ron Helus in the shooting. I believe Chris was in the room when we were officially informed of Alaina's death, yet I can only remember our victims advocate, Andrea, sitting directly across from me and the chaplain. It was all a blur. Chris served the Search and Rescue team and was also a detective, possessing the kind of compassion and sensitivity we needed around sharing details of the incident. We did not want details because they would not help us heal or bring our daughter back. Details would not change the fact that she was dead. We didn't want to be stuck in a mental mind fuck, retraumatizing ourselves because we learned something that would forever remain burned into our mind. That would not be helpful or the healthy choice we needed to make to move forward.

Those details, we believed, would take us down the dark road of "why?" which included many questions that people would continue to ask us over and over. Why did someone not see the shooter's pattern of violence? Why did Alaina go that night? Why was she one of twelve when more than a hundred people were in the building? Why couldn't she have gone the next time? Why didn't Hannah and I encourage her not to go? Why was she the only

Pepperdine student? Why Alaina? The only answer we have is that there is no why that will change the outcome. We knew it then. We know it now.

Chris immediately understood and respected our decision. I could see it in his eyes; he knew what we didn't want to know. He carried those gruesome details for us, and I could never thank him enough for bearing this knowledge. He took protective measures and contacted us a few days before any articles from the local or national papers would appear, or before anyone from the media contacted us, giving us time to absorb the information and respond thoughtfully. He also helped to educate and prepare us for any legal information regarding the police reports. All of this could be overwhelming, but he paced us like a good coach. Above all, Chris and our victim's advocate, Andrea, were the epitome of kind in all our communications.

Frequently Andrea would call and let us know about new information and police reports. She knew we didn't want any details and respected our need to be informed only about whatever was necessary for us to know. She was also prepared if we changed our mind, which we never did. Andrea was impeccable with her word and perfect for her role in our family. These two people were just the first of many who would appear at just the right time, playing just the right role to help us, as if the heavens had orchestrated this entire unfolding of ongoing support.

Nearly six months after losing Alaina, our dear friend Megan, who coordinated Alaina's funeral, reached out to see if Hannah and I would like to meet Matt Maher, the

Christian singer from Nashville who was in town with his band. Hannah loved him and had been to his concert with Alaina a few years prior. Megan wanted to know if she could borrow the bus used for my men's soccer team to give him a tour of the valley and stop at a winery. I thought it was a great idea and knew how much his music meant to Hannah. It had given her so much joy and strength for years, and I had begun to enjoy it too. I offered to drive Matt and his musician friends around town and invited him to join us for dinner later that night at Il Posto. We were planning a large dinner at our restaurant to thank all the people who had done so much for us and it felt great to finally have the opportunity to give back. I asked Megan if Matt would consider singing Hannah's favorite song, "Lord, I Need You," and he said yes. I was so excited knowing how much Hannah would love it.

The day came and I rolled up with the green twenty-two-passenger 2005 Ford Econoline. I was hoping it wouldn't break down on the day and thankfully it didn't. I guess He was on our side. Matt, Stu and Otto (Matt's fellow musicians who have been wonderful new friends thanks to this event), and a few others piled in, and Megan joined me as our tour guide. It was a magical afternoon touring the Napa Valley and we all ended up bonding. My partner at the restaurant, Justin, pulled all the stops and dinner was incredible. Food and wine were flowing, and everyone was enjoying each other's company.

Matt grabbed his guitar and sang "Your Grace Is Enough," "Hold Us Together," and "Lord, I Need You." We were blown away and deeply touched. The music carried so much of the collective emotion and said everything we could no longer articulate in our grief, leaving not a dry eye in the place. Matt quickly became a dear friend whom we could never repay for this moment. Six months later, I would call him to inform him that Addie (Megan's six-year-old daughter) had passed.

Nobody who had gathered that night would have ever in a million years suspected that yet another family would lose a child, but we would have Matt's music to buoy our broken hearts and restore our spirits again. I realized this is how grief worked, knowing that it would eventually give back. This is when I began to understand the equation: Grief respected equaled grace in return. Believing in this process helped me to navigate the abyss it left in our hearts.

Soon, I was finding new relationships like this all the time, growing not only personally in the aftermath of losing Alaina, but also professionally. For years as a small business owner, I had participated in the CEO mentoring group, Vistage, to help me develop skills as a husband, father, and business leader. I appreciated the whole-person approach to this community and had made some great friends. A few months after the shooting, internationally renowned speaker Bob Anderson came to visit our group. In all previous meetings I attended, our fearless leader Paul would let the speaker know that I was a parent of a victim of a mass shooting and that this grief was still raw in our group, but that day, he accidentally forgot.

It turns out that Bob Anderson spoke about emotional intelligence and resilience. Having served in the military, working as a school administrator and holding various other occupations, Bob earned numerous degrees and spoke all over the world. That day he discussed four detrimental fears and needs: the fear of being wrong and the desperate need to be right; the fear of rejection and the need to be loved; the fear of failure and the need to succeed; the fear of showing emotion and the need to appear strong. All these fears and needs are universal, Bob explained, and they resonated deeply with everyone, especially me, as a man who was told to repress his emotions for most of his life.

The fear of being wrong hit home for me. How many times had I realized I was mistaken but continued to argue so that I could prove my point? It almost made me laugh realizing what a waste of energy I had spent trying to win an argument. The fear of failing and needing to succeed also resonated. As a coach with an inherent competitive aspect to my personality, I knew that competition was actually a good thing for my players and would help them improve. When Alex's team was winning, I gently pushed them to go higher even though the parents were saying, "But they are winning." I knew if they had the fear of failure, they would become bored with the sport. I explained to the parents that the only way for the boys to be better was to have them feel challenged. That would ensure their respect for themselves as players and for the sport. It worked. And it connected with the last fear Bob addressed, the fear of showing emotion or the need to appear strong. It was important for me to foster the safety for my players to be vulnerable. It was better to fail at trying to improve than stay safe by not trying at all. This way, everyone could experience continuous growth. I loved how Bob brought all these together, and I felt energized by his insights and wisdom.

After speaking for an hour, Bob was ready to take a break but wanted to share a story about his fiftieth birthday. He was on the East Coast in a celebratory mood, driving his dream car, a Ferrari which he had rented. I assumed he wanted to feel like Tom Selleck as *Magnum PI* but maybe he was more like Chevy Chase in *Vacation*. At any rate, Bob said he was enjoying himself immensely when his wife called to tell him to pull over because she had some news.

Bob felt deflated and a bit annoyed to put his celebration on pause, let alone stop his joyride. But he sensed something huge was about to come out of his wife's mouth and felt compelled to comply, hoping she was okay. As soon as he told her he'd pulled over, she informed him about the shooting at Sandy Hook Elementary. Even the mention of the word "shooting" sent shockwaves through our little group at Vistage. I felt my spine stiffen and could feel everyone's eyes on me as Bob continued with his story. Bob did not know about my experience and our leader did not know he would be mentioning a shooting in his talk. I tried not to move as I focused on his story. I wasn't offended and listened with awe at what he said next.

It turns out Bob Anderson had coached youth sports at Sandy Hook for years, which was only a few miles from where he and his wife had lived for quite a time with their children. Bob understood why his wife needed him to pull over. She knew he was a very emotional individual and cared deeply about the children he coached and everyone else he knew at Sandy Hook. The news of their murder hit him like a load of bricks. He listened to his wife, feeling rage, and he started kicking and slamming his fists into the prized Ferrari, causing some damage to it.

He was sharing this anecdote to illustrate his awareness of emotional intelligence and how his wife was being thoughtful in the way she would deliver the news, which she knew would be deeply upsetting. It was a great story that resonated with me, and I assume many others that day.

After everyone cleared the room at the break, I introduced myself to Bob and offered him a teal green "Alaina's Voice" bracelet.

"Bob, my daughter was a victim in the mass shooting at Borderline a few months back."

He immediately burst into tears, apologizing profusely for telling the story.

I looked at him and said, "No Bob, it's okay. I'm glad you told your story. I don't know why, but I feel we were supposed to meet."

Bob wiped his eyes and shook his head, visibly relieved. Somewhere inside him was a huge bearhug that emerged at that moment, and it would become one of many over the years.

He stepped back after hugging me and wiped his eyes again. I looked him in the eye, reiterating how grateful I was that he shared his story.

"Bob, I cannot live sheltered from other people's stories. We are all sharing in the collective grief of mass shootings and other acts of hate that continue in our country."

He listened. I wanted him to know I appreciated him telling the story and did not want him to feel badly for doing so. He had expressed his emotions in a way that allowed everyone in the room to feel his despair and devastation, which reflected what my wife and I and so many others have felt and continue to feel in our lives. Since then, Bob has become a great friend and helped mentor my public speaking career.

Bob Anderson also helped me see the value of the relationships—and all the emotions they carried—that had quietly shaped our lives. One was with Chaplain Lee Shaw, a steady presence in the Napa community. We first spoke the day we received the call about Alaina, and his calm voice brought comfort we didn't know we needed in the chaos. Lee respected our space while we grieved yet made us feel seen and understood. Hannah and I loved him dearly. When he passed in 2024, the loss hit us hard, yet we found peace imagining him and Alaina together—perhaps forming a friendship in a new form.

While these new relationships were showing up, unexpectedly, changes within existing relationships were offering more opportunities to grow. Our marriage was also undergoing some changes while Hannah and I, individually, were navigating the impact of losing our daughter in a mass shooting. This kind of trauma would stress even the most easygoing couples, which we took great pride in being. In our many years together, Hannah and I have had only a handful of full-on arguments, yet when I decided to get a tattoo, we had one for the record book. Tattoos were not our thing, though we'd seen some of Alaina's friends had gotten tattoos of her name with coffee beans or music or any symbol that reminded them of her. I appreciated the intention behind those tattoos and felt like something was missing for me. I love my wife dearly and have a deep respect for the deliberation that she puts into making big decisions, so it surprised me when she looked at me one day and said, "Maybe we are getting our first tattoos!" We both laughed and cried at the same time, sharing that look—half dare, half denial about the idea—but there was no denying a seed was planted.

About two weeks later, when things were still very blurry in the aftermath, I kept seeing all these tattoos on Alaina's friends and, although I'm not a guy who has FOMO—a fear of missing out—I don't know what came over me. One day after I visited her gravesite, I sensed it was time to get one too. My head and heart were aligned. Now was the time. I drove myself to the Ink Garage, which had made me very uncomfortable in the past.

Of course, the Gods had some interesting timing. Hannah called me to say hi right before I walked in. I felt my cheeks flush and my heart pound. I brushed off her inquiry into what I was up to and made it sound like I was just running around town. I didn't bother to mention I had to get a tattoo now—as if I had just stopped to get gas. Instead, we agreed to catch up at home.

I suddenly found myself anxiously waiting for the next available artist to plunge his needles into me and leave some ink. It was almost surreal and for a split second, I thought I might bail, but my feet were rooted firmly on the floor. A man named Henry finally approached. He was familiar with my story and had done some of our friends' tattoos and had practiced Alaina's signature. He was willing to give me a tattoo right then and there. I looked around, took in a deep breath, slightly terrified. *Holy shit.* This was about to happen.

I asked, "Henry, is this going to hurt?"

"The meaningful ones never do!" he said and chuckled.

I trusted this. What pain could be worse than the one we had already endured?

I sat in his chair, pushed up my sleeve, and let him ink Alaina's name with a single music note on my forearm. I watched in amazement as it didn't hurt at all, yet the process was emotional and fulfilling—until I sent the picture to Hannah and some friends.

I did not expect her reaction. To say my wife was upset is an understatement. Hannah was unbelievably disappointed with me, which didn't sit well. I went slack-jawed. I could feel her anger. Had I done something wrong? Was I being a bad husband by getting a tattoo? I had no idea why this decision could send her sideways when we had already shared a moment, and a laugh, when we first entertained the thought of getting tattoos—after she had mentioned it first. Her response naturally startled me. It was one of those "men are from Mars and women from Venus" moments. Stupefied, I needed clarity.

"I'm sorry love, but why are you upset?" I asked, feeling my heart pound. Deep down I knew. If I didn't know this would bother her, then why did I say I was running around, rather than walking into Ink Garage?

I have always loved Hannah's directness, but I was suddenly terrified because I knew she was *very upset* and she had no trouble articulating that. First, she was upset that I did it without her; she didn't understand that I didn't want to wait. Second, she had called me right before I walked into the Ink Garage and told me she was at Whole Foods. It occurred to me to disclose what I was about to do, yet I withheld the information. Why? Telling her did not feel like it would help my effort in actually getting the tattoo even though that would have been more forthcoming. I guess maybe I was scared shitless that I'd lose the courage to finally do it.

Now what? Even if I realized maybe I should have talked it over with Hannah first, it was a done deal and now a permanent part of my body for the rest of our lives. After thinking through how it would feel when Hannah actually saw the tattoo for the first time, and bracing for her next warranted reaction, I somehow found the courage to start my truck and drive home. I loved what I chose, yet not how I chose it.

Clearly, I knew I was doing something we had not discussed and trying to get away with it. Lastly, and completely understandably, she said, "Arik, we are in a new part of our lives. We can't *not* communicate with one another! We have to tell each other where we are at and what we need or feel!" She was right; we needed to communicate, now more than ever. In hindsight, it would have been less hurtful to her if I had just said, "Hannah, I really want to do this," and explained why. I know she would have supported me. She was right. But the ink had dried. Literally.

Instead, I was definitely in the doghouse. I might have apologized fifty times, as I never ever intended to hurt her, especially when things were so fresh with the loss of our daughter. Yet in that moment of insight after visiting Alaina's gravesite, which allowed me to stay connected to her, I realized that my intention for getting the tattoo was another way to keep that connection every single day. That's all I wanted, with Henry's help and artistry. Some ink and a way to let my little girl hold my hand, or my arm, as if somehow, just maybe, her fingers were part of the ink of that tattoo.

It was a sign that the random tattoo parlor I chose was one that had her signature. All these thoughts were unclear in the blur of those first days and aftermath of her death, but it's now apparent why I was acting so compulsively. I just wanted to stay with my daughter. I wanted to look at my arm and feel her in one small way. I wanted Alaina to stay with me. That said, I could have taken a better approach to communicate this. The tattoo would mark the beginning of my own growth, while Hannah had undertaken her own. We were growing in parallel, not always at the same pace, but always with the intention of supporting each other as we grieved and grew our resilience. We were both learning by allowing ourselves and our egos to get out of the way.

Tattoo tales aside, we were also growing through the many people who would come into our life by happenstance and events we never would have typically attended. One day, Hannah mentioned an authors' signing at the Napa Valley Historical Society. She was a member and attended events from time to time. She loved history. While I appreciated it, it wasn't something I followed and certainly didn't read women's historical fiction, which is why I was surprised when she asked me to go with her to an authors' reading one rainy day in December 2022.

We were in the kitchen making lunch when she popped the question.

"Do you want to go with me to a historical society meeting? It will be a discussion between two women authors on historical fiction."

I stared at her, stunned. I thought, *Is that really a question? Do I have to say yes?*

She nodded and I glimpsed a bit of mischief in her eyes. Of course she was asking me to join her. Since she is my best friend, I replied, "Yes, absolutely! It is a date." Even though I have never been a big reader, we went to Bouchaine Winery in the Carneros region of the Napa Valley on a rainy night to hear internationally bestselling author Kristen Harnisch discuss her trilogy, *The Vintner's Daughter*, *The*

California Wife, and her latest book, *The Vintner's Legacy*, and Debra Green discuss her debut novel, *Convention of Wives*, all set in the Napa Valley.

After we enjoyed some wine and hors d'oeuvres, Kristen and Debra led us through their writing journey with a lot of interesting details about the historical research that went into their books. After the signing, we were saying our goodbyes and I made my way to the authors' table, having no idea I was approaching my future when I asked them both how they started writing and if I could email them to get some suggestions on how I might write this book. I had no idea how to get it on paper yet. Both were very helpful and after they did a bit of background check on my business and Alaina's Voice Foundation, they understood the story I wanted to tell. Debra set me up with the names of some parents who had written books about losing their children. Kristin offered the same and introduced me to award-winning author and writing coach Holly Payne. We set up a Zoom to touch base and explore what her role would be. We hit it off from the moment we were introduced. She's been a great coach, mentor, friend and cheerleader all in one. The words on these pages would not have come to this if it weren't for Holly.

I don't know why some of these relationships have come about and often wonder if they would have happened had our story been different. I honestly wish I never had a reason to meet any of them, yet I feel so blessed to have them in my life now. I would never have started this book if I had not said yes to something new, so different in fact that my son Alex still jabs at me about my attending that meeting and jokes, "You read, Dad?" When he gets to this part of the book, he will know that I read. And I also write. And that his sister's voice gave rise to my own.

I share all this to ponder, what if Hannah and I had a different mindset? What if we were still angry about what happened to Alaina? Imagine how much energy we would have wasted staying stuck there out of some sort of righteous indignation. What if I'd gotten up and walked out of Bob's presentation, or if he had been told I was in the room and changed his speech so that he didn't offend me? What if I hadn't gone with Hannah to the Historical Society meeting when Kristen and Debra spoke? I wouldn't be speaking to crowds about grief, resilience, and post-traumatic growth, and you wouldn't be reading this book. The mystery of it all still overwhelms me.

The point is that we have the capacity to grow from grief if we allow for it. This principle was the key to our recovery and healing. Our *willingness* to allow for growth was the reason we were able to rise above the feelings of anger and blame that very often keep most people stuck in grief, as if those emotions justify a need to lash out at the world, or at God, or both for what happened. Fortunately, my wife and I saw a different way. Together, we reoriented ourselves to growth. I am so grateful that our compass was pointing in this direction because we encountered so many people and opportunities that expanded our lives and made them better. Post-traumatic growth was real, and it was also a choice. Whether we choose to open to new relationships, life possibilities, personal strength, spirituality or appreciation is up to us.

Truth be told, even though the journey of post-traumatic growth has been eye-opening, I would trade it if it meant I could have my beautiful, funny, kind and sincere daughter back. But that is not real. I know this. And I have adjusted my own expectations on what life might dole out at any given moment. I did not want to waste my energy being a victim. I knew I had another path out of my pain. By allowing for new friends and relationships, Hannah and I were evolving as a result of losing our daughter. That is a hard truth, but it is *our* truth. Growth through loss will remain a mystery, yet it is undeniable. I am growing. So is my wife. We want to believe that wherever Alaina might be she is still growing, watching us evolve even in her absence.

Staying Connected
When Falling Apart

IN THE WORST moments, especially at the beginning, Hannah and I could have retreated into our respective corners of recovery like seasoned prize fighters. Away from everyone else, we could sweat out our discomfort, alone, and never risk having the other catch us in a moment of vulnerability. The pressure to be strong during any crisis we might face—be it illness, accidents, death or divorce among countless other pressures—only reiterates the false pretense that we are not allowed to fall apart. That any crack in our armor revealing the slightest weakness is somehow wrong, and in the worst case considered contagious. So we tell each other, "Be strong. Be strong!" as a projection on ourselves—to stay strong for those whose lives are shattering all around us. The thing nobody remembers is that this break*down* is only temporary and will almost inevitably be followed by a break*through*. What if life is meant to break us open? If that's the case, it takes a lot more energy to recover when you're alone. Hannah and I both knew that we would need to stay together while we both fell apart.

    The alternative is being disconnected, which is death to any relationship and the cause of almost every problem no matter the infraction. Learning about the toll of trauma on couples strengthened our resolve to remain connected through our journey, as eighty percent of couples who lose a child end up divorced. That was not an option for us or even a consideration. Hannah and I had always shared a special connection as soulmates. I didn't necessarily believe they existed until I first saw Hannah at Pepperdine my junior year. Then all bets were off. My world was tilted on its axis and has remained there ever since. Hannah would not only give me a compass in faith, she would also become my best friend for life.

    From the moment I met Hannah, something clicked, and I knew on our first date I would marry her. However, because I had some restraint thanks to the wisdom of my buddies, I didn't want to come across like some clingy stalker, so I didn't tell her that for a very long time. I was trying my best to play it cool, chill out, and allow for this remarkable woman to choose me too.

    Alaina loved hearing the story of how we met and was reminded every year when we sent out our Christmas cards. Why? Because I liked to tease her that her mom made the first move. Alaina's eyes would grow wide, and she would giggle because she knew deep down that was far from the truth, but we'd reenact the "meet cute" every year around the holidays.

I explained to my daughter how her mom caught my eye when she entered the Pepperdine Student Government Association (SGA) when I was vice president in the fall of 1994. There was just something magnetizing about Hannah, which made it hard to concentrate during the meeting. I sensed her dynamism immediately. Not only was she smart and sincere, but she was also funny. I tried my best to focus on running parliamentary procedure as if it were any other day in this organization that helped plan activities on campus, run budgets, and communicate with the administration. I'd like to say I was doing a good job, but I was distracted by Hannah's charm.

Before we left for the holidays, there was a Christmas tree decorating event for the students staying on campus. A good-willed glitter fight ensued with multiple students, yet Hannah and I targeted each other. When I was still trying to shampoo the glitter from my hair a week after our obvious "flirt fight," I realized she had won.

A month later, during Christmas break when I was bored at home, missing my friends and all the activities, I decided to send out holiday cards. This was prior to the days of email or social media, and there were no services where you could design a holiday card online and have all the envelopes addressed. Instead, I embarked on a good old-fashioned letter-writing project and wrote more than ninety cards, addressed every envelope with a pen and then stuck on every single stamp. This was a labor of love that took a lot of time, which was the whole point. I needed something to do and wanted to connect with the people I loved and missed.

When I got to the post office and mailed them, I felt good. I didn't expect anyone to write back, but I was elated to find a card from Hannah, wishing me a very Merry Christmas and happy holiday season. We had only spoken a few times in the SGA office, but I was holding a tangible piece of evidence that she had been flirting with me in the glitter fight as much as I had been flirting with her. I was beaming. It was the best holiday surprise of the season, and it gave me the signal to make the next move. Of course, this was an assumption, but a man can hope. I was considering asking Hannah on a date as soon as we got back on campus when the opportunity presented itself.

We returned to help with New Student Orientation in January but found ourselves facing mudslides after the California rains wreaked havoc on the coastal hillsides. Malibu was always in the news and that year was no different. Not only was Pepperdine's campus flooding but mudslides were threatening to bring down the hills. We were told to help or go home but be prepared. As members of the SGA Emergency Response Team, we were asked to recruit other student government officers to help sandbag the campus. Hannah's name happened to be on my list, which back then was called a "phone tree" because automatic alerts did not exist. The idea was that you called the next person on the emergency list to relay the information. When I called Hannah, she told me that she was heading home and could not help. I realized I wanted to stay on the phone with her to get to know her more but had to keep calling everyone else on the list. It was not the time to ask her on a date, but it took everything I had to resist the impulse. I loved talking to her. I loved hearing her voice. I had hoped for better timing, but now was the time to help the Malibu community, not find a way to date the most mesmerizing woman I had ever met.

A few days after the storms abated and mudslides were no longer a threat, students in SoCal began to return to campus. Hannah called to ask about her friend, Lady, joining SGA. Smooth move on her part. Hannah is a smart woman. If she liked me, she did not want to appear too forward, but she needed a reason to call me again. I was happy and relieved because it gave me the perfect opportunity to ask her to go for ice cream at Ben & Jerry's. She said yes and we agreed that I would come pick her up. While I had no clue about dating, I was so happy she created the perfect opportunity for her to learn how I felt. On the way to get her, something seemed different—in a good way. En route to ice cream, we made a detour for Coffee Bean and Tea Leaf for their famous blended iced mocha and a relationship was born. My future wife had a love affair with a coffee drink that would eventually be passed to our daughter. A blended iced mocha would become their ritual to the point that Hannah and Alaina would make sure there was a detour to get the iced drink touting the purple straw with any opportunity that presented itself.

It was so easy to be in each other's company and I didn't want our first outing to end. The funny thing was that we pretty much talked about everything else but her friend Lady joining SGA. I loved her cover. She had set me up so well and I fell for her just like that. Deep down, my soul felt at home with Hannah. I knew something was different about her, yet I also needed to contain my enthusiasm for the future. The following week, I summoned the courage to ask her to a proper dinner and we found ourselves sitting in North Malibu at Coral Beach Cantina, an intimate Mexican restaurant tucked into a small hillside, a short walk from Zuma Beach. We sat at a little booth, fixated on each other, talking and talking, as if we could finish each other's sentences. We shared an inexplicable connection throughout our first meal together. I couldn't wait for her to tell a story, yet I knew what she was going to say. There was a sort of magnetism between us, and she immediately became my best friend. I felt lucky to have the best of both worlds.

We officially started dating later in the semester. One night, a bunch of my friends were going to see a movie in LA called *Higher Learning*. It was a controversial movie regarding racism in a university, yet we considered ourselves cutting-edge college students, of course. I asked Hannah if she wanted to go to the movie. "Who's going?" she asked. I rattled off a list of names: Greg, Dennis, Chris, Brian, Brett, and a few others. She wasn't fazed and would soon become "one of the guys" in many ways. She was at ease with my friends, and they loved her.

When I graduated from Pepperdine in April 1996, Hannah was starting her junior year and would be spending the summer studying abroad in London. While I was happy for her, I was also heartbroken. We wanted to stay connected on a daily basis but there was no social media, no cell phones, and only very slow dial-up connection with the internet, thanks to AOL's "You Got Mail" email application. Other than that, all we had were insanely expensive international phone calls and air mail. However, waiting at least twenty seconds for the dial-up service to connect felt lucky back then and we communicated across the distance in that way. We added handwritten cards to the mix, until Hannah started calling collect so we could hear each other's voices. I was glad to accept the call, which meant I had to pay for the astronomical charges. To make a collect call, you inserted a quarter to get a dial tone, then connected to an operator who would make a call to a landline, where the recipient would pick up and accept the call, which would be billed to them. This was the cost of continuing a long-distance relationship. Even though I was still just a college student, it was worth every dollar to stay connected to Hannah and I loved hearing about her adventures.

When she returned from the UK, Hannah loaded her schedule to graduate a year early and save her parents a ton of money. At the same time, we had been dating over a year and a half and knew marriage would be in the cards someday. Hannah, a Filipina American, had a good résumé and good grades. She applied to nine different school districts to teach yet only received an offer from Napa Valley Unified School District, a convenient location for our relationship. It was evident that someone had a plan for us.

The day she moved with her parents to her new apartment was the day I asked Ernie, her father, for permission to marry his daughter.

We were twenty-four and twenty-three years old when we married in 1998. Two years later, our family began with Alaina's birth on July 27, 2000. We didn't know the gender and wanted to be surprised. I secretly wanted a boy because I was one of two boys. I knew nothing about little girls, yet when Alaina was born, we shared an immediate bond. Hannah and I felt so blessed and filled with so much joy. While the nurses were checking Alaina immediately after birth, I stood by her and she grabbed my finger, and I was hooked. She was so strong and gripped my forefinger in a way I will never forget. We shared an instant father-daughter bond, and I was introduced at that moment to a new kind of love, a force that would change my life forever.

Over the next four years, we developed a special connection that I still draw on when I'm missing her. I can remember the best moments with her and recall the love—and even the exhaustion—of those early years. One of my favorite memories of Alaina was sitting on the couch watching a VHS tape of Donald Duck ice skating on a pond with a bad guy, who drilled a hole in the ice the size of a baseball. Donald, in his skating reverie, didn't know about the hole and skated over it, then fell in until all that was sticking out was his bill. He let out a muted *quack*.

Alaina giggled so hard that I rewound the tape and we watched it again. She couldn't stop laughing, so I rewound the tape over and over. I can still hear her giggling. She was an easy toddler and traveled well on our first family trip to Guatemala to visit my college roommate, Ricardo. We had a great time exploring the little towns and ancient ruins of Lago Atitlan and Alaina seemed to roll with it all. Our love of traveling was firmly rooted in her and would continue to be a constant in our family—taking us all over Europe.

In early 2004, when Hannah was pregnant again, Alaina and I were at one of her favorite restaurants, Hurley's, on a daddy-daughter date, enjoying her favorite pasta with butter, cheese, and shrimp, when she told me she wanted a little sister. Another time, my parents took Alaina to Hurley's for dinner, while Hannah and I came from a prenatal checkup. When Hannah announced she was carrying a boy, Alaina teared up. She said, "I wanted a sister and to name her Aurora Briar Rose Sleeping Beauty." It was hard not to giggle, it was adorable, yet Hannah said, "Laina, your little brother is going to be named Alex, and I am sure you'll be a wonderful big sister."

When Alaina finally realized she would still be a big sister, she couldn't wait to meet her little brother and on April 1, 2004, we welcomed Alex Ernesto Housley to our family.

Sports soon became part of both their lives. I began coaching Alaina's soccer team when she was four. I stopped when she was eleven and the girls on her team weren't taking me seriously anymore, calling me "Coach Baldy." I didn't mind their moniker, yet I knew they needed someone to help them get better and give them a bit of a push. Once I stepped aside in 2011, I continued to help when they needed it because they were so much fun to coach.

Alex would follow in his sister's footsteps. As a toddler, he would wear his soccer cleats or Samba's and uniform everywhere we went for years, so when he finally was old enough to play, he was all in. Soccer would become his greatest passion. Hannah was the head coach of his team for a season. I assisted as much as I could. Alex joined another team during his second year, and I saw it was time to transition to coach him in 2011. This was also part of the decision to step away from Alaina's team after seven years. When Alex was approaching eight years old, I was asked to recruit some of the other players in the recreational program and start a travel team for U9. I took great delight taking Alex and his teammates, Anthony and Sergio, all over the Bay Area for games. "The Three Amigos" couldn't get enough soccer and sometimes played three games per day. When both Alex and Alaina had games, Hannah and I would pass each other in the house, say goodbye Saturday morning, then meet up Sunday night. It was all a whirlwind, but the kids loved it, and we all made some great friends and memories during those years, even though we had to divide and conquer with both kids in sports. The years of soccer fed our love of travel, planting the seed for our son's future when we traveled to England and Wales. Alex had a dream to play there someday.

Hannah and I were not only coaching our children's teams, we were building our own team together, coparenting, navigating the logistics of supporting our children's passions while maintaining our marriage and friendship. We had developed a deep commitment to support our family's ability to flourish, and this foundation would buoy us in the worst of times. We had no idea back then, but our involvement in soccer would become one of the keys to our ability to come together—rather than fall apart—when tragedy struck our family. We knew where the goal post was even on the darkest days when we could barely see any glimmer of hope beyond our grief. We needed to focus on our connection, on finding a way to keep our hearts open to each other—and to everyone else who would show up to greet us on the way to our healing.

The renowned scholar and writer, Joseph Campbell, who wrote *The Hero with a Thousand Faces*, had a great lens on living through failure, adversity, and suffering. He credits Nietzsche for instilling in him an understanding about facing life's greatest challenges, and this resonated with me, Hannah and our son:

"Nietzsche introduced me to the idea of *amor fati*—the love of your fate. Whatever happens, no matter how difficult or disastrous it seems, embrace it as though it's exactly what you need. It may feel like everything is falling apart, but approach it as an opportunity or a challenge.

"When you bring love and resilience to those moments, rather than discouragement, you'll discover inner strength you didn't know you had. Surviving any disaster isn't just about endurance—it's a chance to grow in character, stature, and wisdom. What a privilege that is.

"Looking back on life, you'll see that what felt like your greatest failures or wreckage were actually the events that shaped who you've become. Crises push you to your limits, and in those moments, your true strength emerges."

While nothing could take away our pain or fill the hole in our hearts left by Alaina's murder, we realized it was our choice how we responded, who we allowed into our hearts, and why. We were blessed to have the foundation of meaningful, authentic relationships and the communities they created, which turned out to be the key to finding our way to healing. I realize for so many others it is the hardest thing to say, "This is not happening *to* me, it's happening *for* me." It sounds like New Age bullshit when you're in the throes of such deep anguish, but I was living through hell and simultaneously experiencing the beauty of so much love showing up for us through the network of relationships in all our lives. We survived and found our way to flourish because of this—and it made us stronger and even more grateful. We have been living in a state of grace.

Navigating Grief's Awkwardness

ONE OF THE paradoxes of loss is that it brings us as much love, care and compassion from others as it does awkwardness around grief. Nobody is prepared for bad news. When it hits, we are often so blindsided that we do not know what to say. This is natural. Our emotions become so overwhelming that we literally cannot find the words to express what we really feel. The effect is as if our minds are temporarily paralyzed when so many emotions crash into our psyches. It is no wonder that we can often say some wildly disturbing, or seriously stupid things. I've been there too and said them at awkward times. Now I know why.

After the word was out that Alaina had been murdered, we received many messages of love and support. We also received very awkward messages. The one we heard most often was, "Oh my God, you're kidding!"

And no, I am not kidding that this is what we heard the most. We understood the translation meant, "Oh my God, I can't believe it. That is unbelievable." Similar message, but this one lands in an entirely different way. In the former, who would joke about their child being murdered in a mass shooting? Unless you're going for the worst kind of dark humor, nobody I know would ever take a shot—no pun intended—at such a response. It's clearly the reaction of someone not knowing what to say or perhaps being so terrified of the truth that they literally cannot comprehend it. In this case, when people say, "You're kidding," it's as common a response as when a child laughs at something awful. They simply cannot process the pain and instead resort to another outlet—which is simply an energetic impulse that needs to run its course. But what's not temporary is the pain that these kinds of responses inflict on others, unwittingly, especially those who have lost someone to anything unthinkable. Although I can say I was hurt by these responses, admittedly, I had given similar ones in the past.

One of the worst things I've ever said was when I was young and trying to relate to someone's brain cancer. My message was an attempt to suggest they should live in the moment and choose positivity in day-to-day life. Easy for me to say, right? I was not enduring brain cancer. Though well-intended, my message was not received quite as I had hoped, judging by their facial expressions.

After a dear friend lost a child at birth, I made a clueless, uniformed but well-intentioned comment along the lines of, "At least it wasn't too long to get attached." Really, I made that asinine comment, and I can't imagine the hurt my words caused. It was intended with love but I had been caught off guard. Now, I have a better understanding of how to help people express grief. Sadly, I got a masterclass through my own mistakes, but I now have more compassion for those with less experience. I know it's difficult, if not impossible, to practice for these moments, especially in a society that avoids speaking about grief and is fearful about showing emotion.

The worst message we received, however, was not well-intentioned. I received a standard envelope in the mail one day with a message that looked as if it had been written by a ten-year-old. It was mailed to my office and arrived on my desk. I ripped open a letter written on both sides of a single page. There was no return address or a name on the letter. My hands shook when I read the message: *The Borderline shooting did not happen and Alaina is still alive.* It also alleged that the police department and the government were covering up the whole event. I stopped reading after a few sentences, incensed, and called Detective Chris. He was very apologetic and informed us that a man living in the Bay Area had written similar letters to all the families.

The sender's conspiracy theory was not only infuriating, it felt hateful. He refused to self-identify but insisted on posting the conspiracy all over social media, where we encountered many comments that claimed the shooting never happening. Additionally, that person had chosen to send us a letter by regular mail. We never found out who it was, but I wondered if it had been the work of some foreign bot trying to stir controversy and skepticism about the US government and our society. It was too much to think the sender actually believed what they were saying. The intended harm was obvious, and I found myself wondering if he might be the kind of person who commits these heinous acts of violence.

Other bizarre responses continued to rattle us, such as, "What was she doing so far from campus and at a bar?"

What?

Most people who knew us understood that Alaina was a model student without any penchant for partying. She was extremely diligent, focused on her schoolwork and participating in extracurricular activities that helped her learn a work/life balance. We knew this kind of comment was supposed to help the person understand how Alaina got into that fatal situation. The answer was always a flat out, "She wanted to go line dancing and sing." Just like any other college student who finished their work first and could enjoy campus life. We wanted that for our daughter so she could navigate the world by herself, seeking us only when she needed advice or support for any failure or loss. We wanted to raise an adult, not a child. Alaina had a solid head on her shoulders and did not suffer from FOMA. These well-intentioned though awkward comments after her death only showed how shocked everyone was, struggling to make sense of the senseless.

Still, the awkward responses to her murder continued:

"I know how you feel, I lost my dog recently."

"My grandmother just passed, and I was very close to her."
"Why did you let her go out? I would have never let her go out."

These comments were usually well-intentioned attempts for others to relate to our grief. However, comparison, judgment and criticism did not help us or anyone else, especially in times of need.

Pity was another way people expressed themselves when they did not know what else to say or do. Often, we'd see the "poor you" look on their faces. Or they'd tilt their head and say, "How are you?" I call that the pity tilt. The translation is, "How can you possibly survive this heartbreak?" The intention implies sympathy, yet it comes across as pity. Pity was not something Hannah and I wanted to feel. We were suffering, but we didn't want or need pity. It would not pull us up, which is where we desperately needed to go.

One time in the Napa Target store, a person I knew made eye contact with me but quickly dropped his head and turned as if we hadn't seen each other. I assumed his avoidance was the result of his fear of saying the wrong thing or not being comfortable with showing emotion in front of us. These incidents happened frequently enough for us to see a few patterns in how people respond to tragic events. Some can handle hard. Others struggle. Over time we developed a better understanding and more compassion for the limited capacity some people have to hear bad news. We understand it is very hard to know what to say or how to act.

When we returned to Pepperdine for the memorial in late November 2018, we visited Alaina's favorite clothing store in Malibu. Months prior, Alaina had reached out to me and said she found a sweater that she knew her mom would love and wanted to give it to her for Christmas. She hadn't bought it prior to her murder, yet she was convinced it was "the sweater for mom." I wanted to get it for Hannah from Alaina. I walked into the store with my friend David Roach and found the sweater. The clerk, a surfer with requisite suntanned skin and long hair, said in dude-speak, "What's your name, have you shopped here before?" I replied, "Yes, it's Arik Housley." He typed my name into the database and said, "What are you guys doing? Having a guys' weekend?"

I glanced at David, shrugged, and replied, "Actually, no, my daughter was the freshmen killed in the Borderline shooting and we're down here for the memorial."

David and I shared a glance. I could see David standing resolute with the truth. It was the first time I had ever answered the question so matter-of-factly. The news was still fresh, but David and I could tell the surfer clerk wasn't listening when he replied, "Cool," and continued typing. David and I just stood there dumbfounded. What could we do? Really nothing but try to shake it off. David and I tried to hold back the laughter, and we did until we left the shop. As soon as the door closed, we looked at each other and said, "Cool!" The lesson: Don't ask a personal question if you don't want a real answer. To this day David and I joke about this moment, and it has become a good story. I ended up buying the sweater. I still believe Alaina and I bought that for Hannah, together. Our one last gift.

Not everyone was asleep, numb or insensitive to the news. More often we were met by extreme kindness from strangers. Many said, "I am so sorry, can I just give you a hug?" Prior to losing Alaina, this response would have normally made me feel very awkward. Before, I was not a hugger, especially to strangers, but now I have no issue with it. This was such a simple and kind way to express love and support. Sometimes these hugs lingered. One time a friend, but not a close friend, held me for a solid twenty seconds or more. This was very sweet, and I obliged, but it did feel a bit too long. I thought dropping my arms to my sides would be an indicator that I was done with the hug, but nope, not indication enough. I understood she needed it more than me in the way she was also processing Alaina's murder. It was a strange paradox we discovered—managing other people's grief when we barely had a handle on our own. To this day, we find ourselves navigating this odd phenomenon whenever the subject of Alaina comes up around people we don't know well, and often still, those we do.

This presents an interesting dilemma for Hannah and me. We always wonder how much we should say, to whom, when, and how exactly to say it. It's like we want to set up others to respond with as much respect, love, and compassion as they can. The truth is, it's an ongoing battle and we find ourselves holding back at times, diluting the story.

Withholding information to protect others from the shock of our history is just one path to navigating awkward and sometimes messy communication. Hannah and I find ourselves in conversations wondering if and when to tell people the complete truth when they ask, "Do you have any kids?" We pause, evaluate the situation, and choose one of the following. "Yes, we have a son. He's eighteen." Or depending on the moment, "Yes. We had two children. Our son is eighteen." Usually, the casual conversation will lead to the follow-up question of the second child. Subtlety is a son of a bitch, but it works, sometimes, as a shield, both for us and the person asking. We definitely are not responding to make others feel obligated to ask, so that we can tell them of Alaina's murder. Most often, when they learn what happened, their faces freeze, even though we are not intending shock, just honesty.

One time we were in the San Diego airport trying to find seats. None were available in the waiting area, so we grabbed a seat at the bar. A nice lady next to us started talking, determined to establish some common ground. "Do you have any kids?" she asked.

I replied, "Yes, our son is seventeen."

We spoke a bit about Alex and her kids, then she said, "Do you have any other kids?" I replied, "Not anymore. We lost our daughter in a mass shooting at Borderline in 2018."

She was taken aback.

"Sorry, but you asked and I wanted to be honest with you," I said with kindness.

I could see the sweetness in her eyes and how present she was listening to our conversation. When we parted, I gave her an Alaina's Voice bracelet. She was grateful and equally apologetic in asking the question. I told her she had done nothing wrong by asking the question, but I didn't want to lie. Withholding information felt like lying to me, so when she asked, I came forth. The decision on how much to tell anyone depends on who's listening. If it's the surfer cashier at the clothing boutique in Malibu, I'd suggest not sharing anything. People who are present, who genuinely care what you're saying, usually can handle the full truth like this woman had.

Yet the awkward conveyance of our despair continued no matter where we went. People like to ask the question, "Do you have children?" It never bothered me before, but over time, I developed compassion for those people who chose *not* to have children and have been hearing this question most of their adult lives. During a fundraiser in St. Helena, California, for a mental health nonprofit in the Napa Valley, I overheard the hostess/winery owner ask Hannah, "Do you have any children?" The hostess was simply finding a way to connect with my wife as they were seated next to one another, and we were about to spend the next ninety minutes together.

Hannah replied, "Our son is seventeen." The hostess asked, "Do you have any other children?" Hannah said, "Yes, we had a daughter who we lost."

The woman looked startled and blurted, "Oh God! She wasn't the one who was in the mass shooting, was she?"

Hannah quietly said, "Yes she was." The hostess was very kind in her response. "I am so sorry." She and Hannah continued with a very enjoyable, heartfelt, and sincere conversation. Rather than shut down, Hannah opened her heart and could feel the sincerity and shock in this woman's voice. She wanted to put her at ease and allow her to feel supported in her response. This is where that paradox of having to manage other people's reaction as well as our own continued, but over time, it became habitual for us. Since 2018, these are "normal" conversations for us almost weekly. We always intend to respond kindly, assuming that the person asking doesn't know what they are walking into when they pop the question about kids. It's a fair question to ask, but once told, they frequently don't know how to react. That is okay, it's our normal. We have developed mastery over the years in how we can help others feel less awkward when they learn what happened. There is no use in criticizing them for asking. It's a horrible answer to a very common question and it was up to us to find a way to respond with grace, patience, and sometimes, just a dash of glibness.

Over time, these awkward situations became a lot easier to digest. One day, I saw a customer I had known for years, a wonderful woman. She said, "I pray for you and your family, I am so sorry for the loss of your daughter." I thought that was extremely kind. She then followed it with, "I pray you can have more children?" The smartass in me wanted to say, *I thought we could and if it is a girl we might name her Alaina.* There is my "grief humor" shining through, yet I was a bit taken aback in the moment. It allowed me to realize, we all have a story. Maybe she wasn't blessed with the ability to have children or maybe she was never married. I don't know her story, but I do know she was using kind words to show love at that moment. In hindsight, I sure am glad I knew not to let the inappropriate grief humor slip.

In the spring of 2023, nearly four and a half years after Alaina's murder, Hannah and I were in Whole Foods and saw an old friend. We had not seen each other for years and he was not a bro-hug type; however, when I walked up behind him in the supermarket that day and said "Hello," he turned around and said, "Well hello, Housley. I have not seen you in years! Come here!" and gave me a huge bear hug. It was sincere and an appropriate length of time, and it was perfect. He knew what had happened and contained his questions within the bear hug he offered. It was one of the best ways I had ever experienced someone handling the awkwardness of grief and it would become a model for how I would coach others. It takes a lot of courage to meet another's despair with this kind of open-armed acceptance. The hug was just a way to honor our own courage in navigating the awkward process of losing a child to a mass shooter. His courage to hug us without any other words said it all. His strength helped to grow our own.

Tips for Navigating Awkward Conversations

1. *Keep it simple.* If you can say just one thing, say, "I am so sorry."
2. *Make eye contact.* Words are not always needed. Even saying, "There are no words" is unnecessary. If you have no words, look the person in the eye, smile, and place your

hand over your heart. It's a simple gesture of compassion. Sometimes less is more.

3. *Don't assume you know how anyone feels.* The phrase, "I know how you feel" gets very mixed reviews. You really don't know how I feel or anyone else feels. You know how grief feels for you, but we all have a different story. I don't even know how my wife feels, but I know I love her, and we loved Alaina. I know we both lost our oldest to an act of gun violence, yet she carried Alaina in her womb. I had an amazing yet different relationship with Alaina than my wife. I hurt, too, to this day. I know the hurt Hannah has because I can see it in her, yet I definitely don't know how she feels until she tells me. And sometimes I have to remind myself to ask her and validate her own experience.

4. *Take the initiative to help.* Don't say, "If I can do anything, let me know." In those moments and in grief, it is hard to call and say, "Hey, you said if there was anything. . .well, I would like someone to come over and give me a hug and let me cry on their shoulder or maybe mow my lawn." Most people don't like to ask. My suggestion is to call or message the friend and say, "I have a book to read for the next hour. I am in front of your house. No need to come out, I am happy to be near. If you'd like me to mow the lawn or do the dishes or pick up dinner, please let me know. No pressure, just know I am here if you need me." Many will come out for that hug, talk, cry, or moment. Some may not as they are not ready, yet the message and the act of kindness speaks volumes.

With a Little Faith

FROM THE MOMENT, we received the call on November 8, 2018, I saw an immediate change in my wife. Hannah was drawing from a reservoir of resilience that I never knew existed—only because nothing in her life until then had tested it. Yet she fully confronted it, and I was in awe.

With her first baby and only daughter taken from her, Hannah had many choices in how she could respond, all of them valid. She could have broken down and retreated from me, Alex, and life. That would have been understandable. At times, I wanted to do the same. Grief is a thief with a powerful undertow. Hannah also could have been enraged, blaming everyone, including society, for the horrors her daughter suffered and terror she faced while the shooter fired on her and her friends on a dance floor during College Night. However, denial, anger and blame were not the choices my wife made after her daughter's murder. Instead, she chose to stay open-hearted, compassionate, soft and calm—not only despite her pain, but because of it.

Hannah did not play the victim or the martyr. Instead, she revealed her superpower: the reservoir of resilience within her because of her unwavering faith. I did not possess that kind of faith when we first met in college but learned how to develop it over the years through Hannah's relationship with her Catholic faith. It wasn't a direct path for me either. My parents were not religious in the standard way and had a bad taste in their mouths after witnessing some poor decisions in their churches when they were growing up. My grandpa helped to build a church in the Bay Area. After he had contracted polio and couldn't work, the church leaders informed him he wasn't giving enough money to the church. It was absurd and completely antithetical to Christian values or anything we had read in the Bible.

No wonder my parents shied away from church. At times, my grandparents barely put food on the table with my grandpa incapacitated and my grandma sewing aprons and men's ties to make extra money. My grandpa's colleagues helped them make the rent and pay bills while their own church was hounding them to pay alms. It made no sense and gave them little reason to feel safe in a hypocritical community that prayed on their vulnerability. My parents were no different and shied away from any commitment to a church community, taking us only to a handful of Baptist and Lutheran church services during my childhood, usually when going with my grandparents or my "Aunt" Karen.

Like my parents, I too, was wondering if I would ever find a community that authentically espoused the Christ-consciousness we respected.

I had so many questions.

What drew people to church? Could I ever trust a community to uphold the values that Hannah and I knew existed in the Bible? I was curious and wanted to know more but was confused by everything I had seen growing up around the local Mexican culture in Napa Valley. Everyone I knew seemed to "believe it all," but I was skeptical. While I wanted to believe, I was looking for what was right and what was wrong, because from what I had witnessed, it sure appeared that everyone believed *their* religion was right. This myopic perspective felt limiting to me, especially because I had come to know many intelligent friends whose beliefs varied from Buddhist to Christian to a range of universality mindsets. They each shared a conviction in their faith. But whose was right? My mind stayed stuck in this loop for years.

So how could I know the truth? My friends shared many religious—and anti-religious—mindsets over the years, including Christian, Mormon, Catholic, Buddhist, Atheist, Agnostic and others. Once during college, I attended a Church of Christ in South Central Los Angeles where I felt more welcome than any other church experience in my life. Still, I kept asking God for a "sign" so that I would know which religion was right for me. Was there even a right and wrong religion? I did not yet understand that there was truth in all of them and that discovering what was true for me was the point of my journeying toward a faith that could resurrect me after losing Alaina.

With half a decade to reflect, I came to the realization that religion and faith are not the same. This new thinking represented a monumental paradigm shift for me. It was becoming very clear that each of us is on our own distinct journey, yet we all seek the same end game: to feel connected to each other, supported by each other, and unconditionally loved. I had finally wrapped my head around the truth. My belief structure was just that—mine.

This thinking took time to develop over the years. First, I gained a general understanding of the world's religions and had also learned about cults. I understood why my parents had turned away from an organized church because of the hypocrisy they witnessed. Second, I began to pay close attention to the signs I was receiving, even though many others would call them coincidence. Until Alaina's death, I was one of those people who had to see it to believe it. If I could not touch, taste, smell, hear, or see it then it must not exist. I realize now how limited and arrogant my thinking was. From my perspective, anything that appeared illogical was unproven. Was something real only if *I* saw it? Did I need a trusted source to believe it?

After losing Alaina, my belief in faith wholeheartedly changed. I no longer doubted the signs, or dismissed them as coincidental. The fact that they *were* coincidental validated how they informed me of something the spirit world wanted me to know. Now I fully understand the value of what I saw and experienced, like hearing the music on my phone and seeing the bird in my window. I also believe that Hannah drove through the rainbow that day. It was her experience, and it will remain a beautiful mystery to us both. Old skeptic Arik would have needed scientific validation, especially because I was afraid of being wrong in others' eyes.

Now I don't give two shits about how others might perceive me, not because I am a rebel but because I fully understand that we all have a unique journey which represents our own personal truth in any matter. I can now respect the choice others have to believe or not believe me. I do not need validation from others because I lived the experience. I also am happy if someone is skeptical of my story, and I do not take offense. When I tell the story of waking up one night and feeling Alaina fully in my presence, I can see the doubt in some people's eyes. But I vividly remember that dream. I woke up in the middle of the night a few months after Alaina's death. She had come in to say "Goodnight, daddy" like she sometimes did, but this time, she didn't say a word. Instead, she gave me a squishy hug as I was laying on my back.

As I awoke, I teared up at having felt her embrace while I slept. It was my experience. It was as real as I remember when she was alive. No matter if it was imagined to some, it gave me joy and a reminder of how much love Alaina brought to our lives. I don't need any data to prove that joy. I felt it and I still carry it with me to this day.

Ironically, right when I was working on this part of the book, I saw an interview on *The Late Show with Steven Colbert* with Matt Damon where he described a hug he received from his father after he had passed in 2017. He then went on to describe how it felt like the first hug he had ever received from him when he was a baby. Damon explained that this same preverbal feeling of being held happened again months after his father's death. It was a fully somatic experience for Matt Damon, just as it was for me. We did not question what we felt. We were both held by those we dearly loved and lost. This is faith. This is hope, and this is love.

Evidently, my daughter was hard at work eroding my skepticism, and probably highly entertained by the battle I had waged trying to resist all the signs that she was there, and would always be there, if I remembered to call upon her, to keep talking to her, to engage her spirit in a daily dialogue that allowed her to still exist within our lives. It makes me smile and sometimes cry, yet it always makes me feel her love.

I was on a huge learning curve, realizing that losing the people we love the most can lead us to an inflection point. We either ignore the signs that beg us to look up from our phones or see what the world is trying to tell us and how it might be trying to guide and protect us, if we allow for that grace. I was finally seeing the signs. My brain was changing. My faith in a higher power was being fortified through my years-long journey with grief, while my wife patiently held space for it to happen. I envied and admired her unwavering faith that our daughter was with God and that God was with us. And that God was love. I need a little more time to catch up. Not sure I ever will, but Alaina has left a great trail.

Despite her strong faith, Hannah never pushed others to believe. She has always had a quiet respect for others, yet a firm belief in her own heart and mind about her relationship to God. She never pressured me to become Catholic; however, when we got married in 1998, we were required by the Catholic church to go to Engaged Encounter, a course that prepares couples for marriage. We shared a lot of laughs with other couples and had great conversations. Ironically, Engaged Encounter was where we first met Megan and Jason Dominici, our dear friends who helped organize Alaina's funeral and who would also tragically lose their own daughter, Addie, one year after Alaina's passing. The Catholic church also introduced us to Father Alvin, a Filipino priest, who officiated at our marriage and would baptize and later bury Alaina.

Like Hannah, her family was respectful of my experience with the church and never tried to push anything on me. Both her sisters and their husbands had their own life journeys with faith. They allowed me to be me but also encouraged my growth during those intense years after losing Alaina. Their close family became a safe harbor for me, and I grew to understand that no matter what happened in our lives, they would be there to help us. Both my brothers-in-law, John and Matt, offered insights about their own faith journey and Christianity during the tough first year after Alaina's death. Hannah's older sisters, Leticia and Theresa, immediately traveled to Los Angeles when they heard the news and were there for Hannah and all of us every step of the way. What we called the seven cousins had become six overnight. While the devastation was palpable, it would be assuaged, slowly, over time, through our family's tight bond.

Being welcomed into a large Filipino family like Hannah's would become the first step in my journey toward faith—offering a more formal way to practice it. My family was small, with just me and my brother, my parents and grandparents. We rarely had more than six people at dinner, but I remember a fifteen-passenger cargo van arriving with Hannah's extended family, during our wedding weekend. We had more than thirty Filipinos in our house. I found kids in my closet while others ran around. It was crazy fun. The *titos* and *titas*, *lolos* and *lolas* were all mingling. I could only picture a clown car with all of them piling out of the one vehicle. I loved that they would choose to get one hotel for thirty people if it meant they would be that much closer to each other. They greeted me with so much love and laughter, and it always felt so good having them around. I loved how welcoming they were to me. This is the exact feeling I had been looking for in a faith community. One of belonging.

Over time, one of the most powerful balms we shared was their sense of humor. Every time we visited them in Chicago, the *titos* would say, "Arik, you want McDonalds?" Sensing they wanted me to say yes so that they could get out of eating their traditional food, I would reply, "I eat more Filipino dishes than the kids." We would all laugh as they saw me trying *dinugan* and the other dishes that many non-Filipinos wouldn't eat. Later they would ask, "Arik, you want to go to Hooters?" I never understood this offer, but it always made me chuckle. We didn't have a Hooters where we lived and I had never been, yet I knew the premise after watching the movie *Big Daddy*. Their insistence on going to Hooters started to make me a bit uncomfortable. One day, I finally asked Hannah, "Why do they ask if I want to go to Hooters?" She told me with a wink, "*They* want to go, and you are their excuse." The next time they offered, I said, "Hell yeah, let's go to Hooters." The look on their faces was priceless. It was even better when Hannah said she wanted to go with us, and she did. Finally, after all those visits, I had said yes. They were so excited; it was as if they had won the NBA Finals.

Filipino hospitality eased our suffering after Alaina's passing and our house was full of food for weeks. When Hannah's family visited, they put themselves to work, which I came to learn is a very Filipino offering. They also like to leave us with a lot of food. Rather than give us a few bags of chips, we're given a fifty-count box. They also like to stock us with napkins, frozen meatloaf, and much more. They can't help it. Filipinos love to give. When they visit us in Napa, Hannah's father does yard work, dawn till dusk, and her mom organizes and cleans the house, offering some kind of service project each day. They are extremely giving and kind. Their love language is an act of service. Just be careful if they ask you to go get napkins at McDonalds. What you think might be one or two napkins means as many as possible. If you don't understand that, ask a Filipino friend to explain. Once when Alex had a soccer tournament near their home in Corona, they invited 15 of his teenage teammates over to eat and shower before their flight home. And in keeping with Filipino tradition, they had enough towels for everyone.

With that kind of stability and presence, it made sense why Hannah's faith had such a strong foundation and would become the backbone for us in the wake of our daughter's passing. It also made sense how and why my wife could lead us in the wake of our trauma. She had something bigger than her grief to remind her that there would be more light after the darkness. I know it sounds cliché, but it was so true. Resilience, as Hannah was teaching me—and what I was also teaching myself—was not something you can will. Resilience comes from within and is built upon the foundation of faith. Hannah and I never talked about how we were able to keep going as we did in the midst of our hell. Resilience did not mean the absence of our pain; it meant that we had the capacity to transcend it with the help of our friends and community.

This is a strength I would have never imagined. Most of the time, two things happen after extreme tragedy for couples. It pushes them closer or tears them apart. Our loss of Alaina has made us closer than I could've ever imagined. I never could have gotten through a single day without Hannah by my side. While our relationship with each other changed, it is all the more enriching, expansive. and fulfilling. We like to think Alaina is proudly taking credit for that, too.

One day a few months after Hannah returned to teaching in the spring of 2019, she faced some challenges that proved very emotional. She was overwhelmed by how much she had to do and her spinning head brought her to tears. Her brain had been changed by the trauma. (It's not something most people know to even track, but the book *The Body Keeps the Score* helps trauma survivors understand just how impacted the brain is and how much it actually changes after tragic events.) Hannah was leaving the post office and when she got into the car, tears streaming down her cheeks, the radio came on to "Lord, I Need You" by Matt Maher. Hannah smiled and thought, *That's good timing.* As she pulled the SUV out of the lot and headed east to go home, a rainbow appeared immediately in front of her and she drove through it. For a few seconds, Hannah was surrounded by all the colors of the world, in beauty and in love. We both believe He and Alaina were behind this.

With tears in her eyes, Hannah spoke out loud, "I hear you." That is my wife. Forever stable in her faith. And a rock to me and our son. There are many paths people can take after losing a loved one, especially a child. Hannah exemplified responding with kindness, compassion, an open heart, and even humor. Everything I saw about her the day she walked into the student government meeting played out day after day of our marriage and her dealing with losing our daughter. She would never say she is an inspiration, but she is and continues to be to the many people we have met, and have yet to meet, who need to see how she faced the unthinkable. She would tell them, "I have faith and Him in my life."

Hannah has also become very deliberate in her words. The post-traumatic growth that she gained through our loss has been very obvious to me. Sometimes, what would seem to be a simple text becomes a five-minute decision over word choice. This intention to be precise is important to Hannah. I have picked up some of this trait as well after seeing her in action. At first it was frustrating when I was trying to get things moving again and keep up with the pressures of life. Yet now I appreciate Hannah teaching me this unintentionally. She values quality over quantity. She values preserving the connection between us no matter what is happening in our days. Never in my life could I have imagined our relationship stronger. Hannah has been an inspiration for me to keep a positive mindset and truly helped open my mind to faith and hope. Alaina is witnessing this growth and smiling, I am sure.

Growing the Mind

CULTIVATING THE FORTITUDE to handle Alaina's murder oddly began years before she was even born. My early childhood had given me the opportunity to develop an approach to life that would help me handle all the stages of grief in a way that did not destroy me—but instead helped me to grow. You could say Alaina's death put a new compass in my hand. Losing her changed my mindset, and I have come to understand that sometimes things have to happen to us to spark the kind of change necessary for us to grow. Over time, I have come to realize that these things are not happening *to* us. They are happening *for* us. And how we face them and metabolize the pain is directly related to the puzzle of every experience we've lived until then. The whole tragedy of the shooting forced me to see my past as the ramp up to my evolution. Seeing new possibilities like this is an aspect of post-traumatic growth when open-mindedness steps to the forefront.

First, I was not averse to exploring death. From an early age, I had an odd affinity with cemeteries. I would walk through them and wonder about the stories of the people whose remains lay beneath. My brother and other family members would always ask about my fascination, questioning this very strange preoccupation. Wasn't it creepy for a kid to walk among the dead? No. It actually wasn't. In fact, I felt like death and the afterlife were something I could accept when my day came. I understood death as a natural part of life. Call it unusual, but one day we found a baby jackrabbit in our vineyard which one of us on a tractor had nearly run over. Naturally, we were concerned the baby was alone, and there was no mother to be found. We called a local veterinarian and then attempted to raise the jackrabbit for a while, naming him Jack. We bought Jack all the stuff, too, a cage and water bottle, rabbit food pellets, and straw to keep him warm and comfortable.

Then one day, Jack died, and I was the one who went to the cage to get his remains. It did not scare me. I felt called to duty. I was seven years old but remember feeling a responsibility to care for Jack as deeply as the day we found him alone in the field. I don't know why this felt so natural for me. Maybe I had a connection to the spirit world. I don't know. But I know I was not afraid. It felt more instinctual to interact with life this way—and to respect the afterlife too. At the same time, my brother and father were not super keen to take care of Jack's remains, so it took the youngest

Part Two | THE THINKABLE | 217

to step up. I love how Matt Damon once was asked to describe the afterlife and he simply said, "Home." Maybe that is the odd comfort I had always associated with death. And why I was not afraid. I knew that we're all going home, someday. Some sooner than others.

I often wondered if my strange childhood fondness for cemeteries was preparing me for Alaina's murder. I grew up in a very small family with just my parents, brother, and my father's parents who lived nearby in the Agua Caliente area of Sonoma, California. We shared a family business for as long as I could remember. While Mom and Dad were constantly working, they always made time for us and were unbelievably giving and supportive. My dad worked long hours but found time to coach or be present for us. Dad was even known to have fallen asleep at a stoplight after working thirty-six hours straight in our local family-owned grocery stores, which he and my mom started in 1976 when I was just shy of two. Rumor has it that I'd run down the aisle with my diaper at my knees, triumphant after going to the bathroom. Fortunately, surveillance videos were not common in the mid-seventies. I guess I had an early need to get rewarded after growing up in an entrepreneurial family, where the work ethic carried into the house too. We always had jobs at home. When I turned fourteen, my friends quickly caught on to my dad making us work and declined invitations to sleepover knowing he'd wake us all up by 7 a.m. to bring down firewood or wash the cars on Saturday morning. There was no sitting around playing video games. This was my normal; working and taking care of what you had was an important trait instilled in us. Our family built a reputation of caring for oneself and for the community, so when we faced so much loss, the legacy of our love came back to support us. We had shown up for years as a family, serving our neighbors, and they showed up for us. We would never have gotten through Alaina's death without their help and involvement in our healing. This is the instinctual nature that made me want to help the McGovern family after 9/11.

Our community had faced a lot of loss—from fires to earthquakes and the untimely death of too many youths. Grief seemed to be a frequent visitor for me. From a young age, I witnessed a succession of losses that mapped sorrow across my childhood. However, each of these encounters made me aware of life's uncertainties. They were also the markers that guided me toward an understanding that despite the inevitability of loss, the human spirit has the resilience to endure and somehow find solace despite the pain. These things were beginning to settle into my understanding of the way life is, and in a sense, began building the kind of neural pathways that would lead me out of the despair trap and into a healthier way of grieving.

My next encounter with death happened when I was just eight years old. My parents received a call at our home informing them about the loss of my friend Jake, who was also the grandson of my father's business partner. I remember standing there in the kitchen, watching my mom grip the phone, her face ashen, emotions flowing. My mother swayed, disoriented by the shocking news. The disbelief, tears and sudden absence of my good friend left an imprint on my young mind. Jake was riding his bicycle and was struck by a car. He ended up in a coma and was put on life support but passed soon after. The accident happened not far from where I spent every day in our Yountville store. The tragedy was both incomprehensible and a source of newfound fear for my own safety. My parents worried. What if Adam or I got hit too? Nothing felt safe to them, yet I was unfazed. My entire sense of safety should have shifted but oddly didn't. Losing Jake left me questioning for weeks. However, I felt unusual comfort that he would be okay.

Following Jake's passing, my brother and I were mandated to wear bulky bike helmets as a precaution—and a tangible reminder of life's fragility. Despite the discomfort, the helmets were symbolic guardians against potential tragedy, a measure taken out of love and concern by my parents. If only the helmets could guard against the passing of others. Three years later, my grandfather lost his life to cancer. His death devastated me because he was such a significant influence on my life. As a man who had faced adversity and triumphed, his stories, particularly those about meeting my grandma and the challenges they faced, were a source of inspiration throughout my childhood. Life dealt another blow when he began his battle with cancer and endured multiple heart attacks, ultimately succumbing to his illnesses when I was just eleven.

Witnessing my grandmother's struggles after my grandpa's passing added another layer to my understanding of grief at a very young age. Her pain manifested in heavy drinking. She loved my grandfather so much and his pain devastated her. She felt helpless and turned to drinking for years before and after he had passed. However, she inspires me to this day through her strength as she found a way out of her addiction to stand resolute with family. We were all shocked to see how strong she was in the face of her pain. One day, she quit drinking on her own.

My parents encouraged her to get help for years, but I believe her faith in God helped her stop. What was even more impressive was her ability to be served a glass at a dinner or event, and she could either have a sip or nothing at all. She showed such strength. Her determination to get healthy was my first introduction to resilience and something I would draw upon when I faced more tragedy throughout my school years, continuing the strange sequence of loss.

When I was in seventh grade and two weeks into a "serious relationship" with my first crush, I was introduced to her friend Amy. A few days later, news hit our middle school that Amy was missing. The following day, Amy's body was found; she had been kidnapped and murdered. Shortly after, I would learn that my friend Jose, who was on my youth soccer team, and who coincidentally went to the same elementary school as Amy, was struck and killed by a car while riding his bike home from middle school. It was surreal to be so young and hear this reality of life. My twelve-year-old brain was taking in so much and my heart was broken.

A year later, our family friend Cathy, who was three years older than me, died in a car accident. Cathy's dad and my dad were good friends. We had been on our family boat with Cathy and her family the week before. She and a few friends left school on Ditch Day and were headed to the beach in a caravan. Two of the cars clipped bumpers and the vehicle Cathy was riding in went over the center median, flipped, and landed on another oncoming car. At first glance, Cathy looked okay to the paramedics, yet her internal injuries took her life at the scene. I was devastated. How could all these people full of promise die so young?

The abruptness of these losses shook the foundations of my understanding of life, leaving me grappling with the notion that nothing is guaranteed. Change was inevitable and tragedy was part of that change. When we're young, we think we're invincible, but I was quickly learning the opposite. Life was painting a vivid picture of its uncertainties and forcing me to see that despite loss, the human spirit is wired to endure and even restore itself. It was a brutal cycle, but I slowly began to accept this reality. Years passed, and life continued its unpredictable course. I might have more stories of grief at an early age than the average person, yet each and every experience and person that I lost in my life also made me who I am today. Even more so, it built a greater understanding of our interconnection and ability to grow and heal. With every loss, I learned. With every learning, I grew stronger. With new strength came a new mind. And with a new mind, I had the awareness and ability to face the greatest loss of my life.

November 2018 flipped our world on its head and changed me forever. My mind has not only changed but so has my behavior and responses to my environment. Once the guy who needed to be "right," I do not need to win that game anymore. I need quiet at times. When there is too much going on around me at work, I can't focus. I struggle with crowds and not because I'm worried about a mass shooting. It's more about energetic overload. My entire system is more sensitive than it's ever been, and I need to respect this shift. When we go to a large event, every noise distracts me, yet I try to be respectful of the person with whom I am speaking.

I no longer wear my Apple watch. I prefer to be present with the person I'm conversing with versus distracted by every notification, ping, zing and whiz. Am I really in the same conversation with you if I'm getting messaged every other second? No. I'm not. I want more presence, less pretense. More time to process, fewer distractions. More space. Less chaos. I am even more deliberate now with my actions and responses, taking a page from Hannah who is very careful to use her words only to communicate openly, kindly, and honestly. And I keep changing.

I am no longer trying to fix everything. I used to try to fix every relationship, calm the waters between others, and be the peacekeeper. Now, I have learned to let certain people come into our lives and let others go. I've learned to listen to others and know my opinion isn't the only approach to doing things. I am learning to listen more and talk less. I used to have a habit of unintentionally one-upping the other in a conversation. I am learning to trust in others, know that things will never be perfect, and let others learn on their own accord when they are ready and willing to do so. This was a difficult thing for me to be aware of at first. Self-awareness took a while for me to cultivate, and now I am very aware when that is lacking in others, yet I can have compassion for where they are in their own evolution.

We have intended to make our home more of a safe haven than ever, especially after a long day at work. As a family, we return from the chaos of the world and enter our home anticipating the calm that sets in. Our black lab Scout brings joy and love to our life and our house. It's a safe space where we don't feel any expectations or judgment and we can let down our guard. With all these changes, we continue to stay connected even as we continue to grow through our grief—two budding flowers that find a way to grow through the cracks of a broken sidewalk and remind the world there is beauty to be had and life to be lived and memories to hold and cherish.

How is this possible? Humans have reservoirs of resilience. We are incredibly capable of adapting. And we have choices in every moment that require us to change. The Covid pandemic showed that to many of us and, for better or worse, fell right into the middle of our recovery. We will keep growing. Change is the only constant, perhaps the one certain truth of life.

I did not seek the strength that Alaina's death built in me, but it was there for me to develop. I know she would be proud of me, her mom, and her brother, seeing how we've continued to say yes to life—not just for her, but for ourselves. Alaina is there between every instance. In the space between our words and between our breaths. Her spirit is here. With us. And in our hearts. That makes it possible for us to keep living without her in the way we once loved.

We accept that and we celebrate how far we've come since losing her. It feels like this whole experience was a recipe that has been in the making since first losing Jake when I was eight years old. Each instance, each story, each death, and each relationship has made me into the man I am today. I say thank you. Sometimes it sucks ass, but in the end, it is love, so thank you.

Living Without Fear

OF ALL THE transformations I witnessed in myself, my wife, and our son in the aftermath of our daughter's murder, I did not expect to see her younger brother emerge as a leader. As a teenager when Alaina died, Alex was reserved and tended to stay hidden around others he didn't know. He was always an engaging, funny kid with plenty of healthy friendships from the soccer field to school. He had a life distinct from his sister, but her passing seemed to accelerate his growth the most. Hannah and I could never have predicted that he would leave the country when he was 18 to follow his dream of becoming a professional soccer player.

The decision wasn't ours. Alex was an adult and we wanted to empower him, not coddle him in the aftermath of the tragedy. Many people questioned how and why we could have ever let him go, but it wasn't our right to keep him at home under our constant watch. It was our moral responsibility as his parents to support his dream. We loved him and trusted his choice. We had to let go and trust God that he would be safe, even though we knew that life offered no guarantees.

How could we do that? *Why* would we do that?

A desire to start fresh is common for many who endure so much tragedy. The opportunity to live in a community that is not familiar with the story can appeal to many on several levels. In our case, Alex's need predated his sister's passing. Our son had a dream. After trying baseball and even basketball as a kid, Alex came to love soccer so much that he wanted to be a professional. He knew it was a long shot, yet why not dream big? After traveling often as a child, he began to consider the possibility of playing in England. Leaving us was going to be a natural part of his development. He was naturally differentiating from us, despite Alaina's murder. He was a normal, healthy teenage boy in need of his own life. Prior to leaving for York St. John University, Alex drove a Ford Escape, which he at first named "Ford Escape My Parents," and later christened, "Ford Escape My Dad." Enough said, right? We couldn't help but laugh at his smart-ass comment. I'm convinced he gets it from his mother, but we all know the truth. My son needed me to remove the leash once and for all.

Alex was ready to have a life, and I was ready to trust he could handle whatever came his way. Soccer had taught him resilience. When he was young and I was coaching him and his buddies, he got worked up when his teammates or opponents broke the rules. Being an ardent rule follower, these infractions upset him so much that he'd have at least two meltdowns each game. As his coach, I had to teach him how to flow with these moments so that they didn't threaten his own performance. One day, when he seemed especially sore after being body checked during a foul, I crouched down and looked him in the eye. "Are you injured or hurt?" He stared at me with his huge brown eyes and blinked back a tear. I continued, my voice more stern than usual. "If you're injured, you need to come off the field now. If you're hurt, brush it off and keep going." Alex took that literally after Alaina died. He was not injured. He was hurt, and although that pain would last for years, he could and would keep going. That's Alex.

As his coach, I was able to observe a lot of his developing traits in a way that most parents can't when they only see their kid at home. On the field, Alex was a combination of grit, determination, and perseverance after being the smallest kid on the roster for most of his life. The fact that he made the roster was enough to give him the confidence he needed to pursue his love of the game. When he was really young, Alex and his two amigos, Anthony and Sergio, found themselves in my truck every single weekend on the way to multiple games all over the Bay Area. These boys loved to play and would travel from Santa Rosa to Marin and Napa in a day without complaint. They loved it and wanted more and more time on the field.

Alex was showing up to the game with everything he had, but as his coach, I found myself being super careful never to show any favoritism, which can easily frustrate parents and players alike. As the coach, I wanted to remain neutral and objective and make the best decisions for the whole team. When Alex rose to the top five players on the team, I rarely started him and/or often selected him as the first to sub out. One day a coach I respected, Coach Sweeney, had a talk with me. "Arik, it is not fair to Alex. You're so busy trying not to be the coach that favors his son, it is hindering his development." He was right. I didn't want to be the dad playing his son more than he deserved. I didn't want his teammates to say to him, "You're only starting or playing because your dad is the coach." That day I chose to look for another coach to take over. I would still manage and stay involved, but Alex and the boys deserved the next step. We asked Coach Sweeney to take over, and it was the best decision I ever made. I had to trust that kind of wisdom when it came time to say yes to Alex's decision to play in England.

His dream only intensified throughout middle school and high school. When it came time to look at colleges, he realized the US system did not support the development of professional soccer players. So, after spending two years playing MLS Next as the team captain and earning a 4.6 GPA but finding no colleges that offered what he needed, Alex began to consider his options.

During junior year, he learned about a program in England coached by former professional players. I was interested too, after we looked closely at the financial commitment. University in the UK is a three-year program for a bachelor's degree. Similar programs in the US require students to take many courses they've already mastered, just to add another year of requirements and another full year of tuition. And unlike the NCAA, it put no limitations on playing outside of college. Alex could graduate in three years, not four, and save a boatload of money. By attending university in England, he'd save 25 percent on tuition, an entire year of life, and would not have to repeat any classes he had already aced.

The UK looked like a viable option for Alex's college education. So in January 2022, we flew to England to check out York St. John University. He was admitted in March to play when the i2i Academy put his commitment post on Instagram, introducing Alex as their new player. It was well-deserved and he felt so good about his achievement. He had spent many hours daily in the backyard training on his own or with friends outside of practices. Even after practice, he would put in another two hours in the backyard with the floodlights on every night. He trained through Covid on his own every single day. His drive and determination showed us he had everything he needed to thrive in another country, halfway around the world from us.

As the departure time approached in the summer of 2022 and we scrambled to get everything he needed, including a delayed visa, we finally arrived in England on September 22, early enough to get him to training the very day he landed. He was ready to dig in and make the most of this opportunity. Not just for himself, but for his sister. She would have been urging him on, and he knew it. Her passing did not deter him from his dream. It was as if he had a soul contract with Alaina to pursue it with all the love in his heart. Despite some travel snafus getting to the UK, we managed to get a cheese steak in the airport and give Alex just enough fuel to literally hit the ground running.

    A coach picked us up at the train station the next morning and drove us in a van to Alex's student housing. After Hannah and I dropped off our stuff at an Airbnb, we headed over to his place to give him a hand. Although we knew he would be organized and love setting up his room in his own way, he had a pressing question: Where should he hang his Chelsea FC flag? This was important stuff along with getting him a few new towels. During this time, our Welsh friends, the Hughes family, came to visit, which added another element of familiarity. Alex had known them from the age of three and from several trips we had taken together over the years. The Hughes family would provide a safe haven for him when we were so far from home, and that might have comforted us more than him. He was ready to be free of us, in the best of ways.

    When the day came to say goodbye, I could feel the emotions building all morning. I tried my best to show my poker face, but Hannah and Alex were on to me. When things got too sentimental, we jokingly called our watery eyes "allergies." It was a high pollen–count day.

    As the moment approached for us to leave, I could feel the tightening in my throat and the sting in my nose—knowing it was just seconds before my eyes would water. My heart felt like it was about to explode. Alex was feeling it too and we looked at each other, wiping what appeared to be some damp eyes, and muttered again, "Damn allergies!" I gave him a bear hug after I let him go, wiped my eyes on the sleeve of my shirt, then finally said goodbye to my son.

With the goodbyes behind us, Hannah and I headed to the train with the unspoken looming between us. The last time we had said goodbye to our daughter, we never saw her again. Hannah and I did not talk about this, but we both were thinking it and feeling it. What was there to say? As the train moved on and we grew farther and farther from our Alex, his dream was coming that much closer. It was an odd paradox. Despite waves of pain, we also felt the pride of letting him go—to build new memories and opportunities to explore his potential. Alex deserved this opportunity. He had worked so hard. It was time to take his best shot at becoming a professional athlete while pursuing his degree. He would never live with the regret of looking back on his life and saying we held him back. Letting go was hard but the only right thing to do.

Has the distance between us been difficult? Absolutely. But we know he is doing what he loves and would not have the same opportunity here. Hannah has said to me so many times how proud she is of our son to take this step, even though so many others still question us or more so don't understand how we could let him go so far. Alaina was not as far but we still could not protect her. Alex was doing what he loved and that mattered the most. Trying to control unforeseen circumstances, we have learned, is futile.

I had never been so close to jumping off a cliff, but saying goodbye that day pushed us all to our edge. It was one of the most powerful moments of our family's growth—and one that still defines us. There we were, still tinged with grief, finding the courage to move forward. Day by day. Inside our embrace was our faith—a forcefield so huge it would hold us up forever. This was our threshold crossing, and I swear as soon as we let go, Alaina took hold of our hands. We did not fall. Instead, we had found our wings, and in doing so, were learning to live without fear.

Be the Positive Change

ON THE SATURDAY after Alaina's murder, I was interviewed at Black Stallion Winery, where a make-shift studio was set up with TV cameras from a national network. Hannah wasn't ready for an interview. I was not exactly in the headspace for any media attention either. Besides, I sensed that the reporter was more interested in getting to my brother, Adam, and his wife, Tamera Mowry-Housley. Yet as Alaina's father, I wanted to show my pride for her and sorrow for her loss, and so agreed to the interview. Sitting between Adam and Tamera, I noticed they handled the interview well, and I appreciated their love and support. I believe Tamera held my hand through the entire interview. I don't remember most of the exchange except saying this at one point, "Mark my words, Alaina's voice will be heard."

A few days later, we learned about a GoFundMe account set up in her name. We knew nothing about it and immediately believed it was a scam, so we jumped onto Facebook to tell everyone to stop funding it. Sadly, we learned, it was not uncommon for scammers to set up a fake account to profit from a bereaved person's loss. Fortunately, we were surprised to learn this one wasn't fake. We were relieved to learn that Alaina's suitemate at Pepperdine, Melanie, had started the GoFundMe account to help our family. She was apologetic, wishing not to cause any confusion, and helped us manage the situation. We asked Alaina's godfather, Jake, to help us set up the required legal documents, which then birthed Alaina's Voice Foundation.

Writing a mission and vision statement for any organization can be daunting and laborious, yet once again we were blessed with a guiding light. The minute that Alex, Hannah, and I sat down at the kitchen table, surrounded by family pictures on the walls, the ideas started to fire. I figured it would take a while to come up with the right words until Hannah had a suggestion. "I like the quote from Ghandi," she said. "Be the change you wish to see in the world." Boom. We looked at each other and laughed. That was easy. We agreed to choose a positive phrase and our vision became: *Be the Positive Change.*

The next cognitive challenge was articulating the mission. I wasn't sure it would be as easy as the vision. We started to hash out the values that mattered to our family and were the hallmark of Alaina's life: kindness, education, music and mental health. We agreed that music shouldn't come before education, which sounded like music education. This exercise ended in less than a half hour when we stood from the table with our vision and mission: to spread hope and kindness through education, music, and mental health initiatives. Done. This happened so quickly and felt so right, it was as though Alaina was guiding us through it. In many ways, I could feel her presence with us at the table, urging us to keep the momentum going.

I felt my entire body fill with a pulsing energy. I felt activated, ready to *do* something, do *anything* to help the entire country face this issue of gun violence, not by taking on gun control, but instead focusing on creating a rallying cry for more kindness and mental health support. I believe if the shooter had received support, things might have gone differently. None of us will ever know the answer to this, but I was ready, eager, and willing to be the positive change.

Maybe I was exhibiting a zealot's approach because Hannah and her wisdom gently laid out the reality of my aspiration. "Arik, even if we raise $1 million, it will only go so far in Napa Valley. Imagine trying to spread that amount around the country? Let's focus on our community and try to make a bigger impact right here." As always, Hannah was the voice of reason, and she was right. Napa County has remained our focus for Alaina's Voice Foundation.

With the birth of our family's foundation, we reached out to Hannah's close friend, Stacey Dolan-Capitani, who runs the Napa Valley Wine Auction and referred us to meet with the Napa Valley Community Foundation. The three of us met with the director, Terence Mulligan, to get some advice on honing our focus and building a board. It would have been easy to ask my parents and our close friends Lorrie, Dave, Kristi, and others, who would've been great support as board members, but in order to have the greatest impact and create the most change, we had to think strategically for the foundation.

Terence advised us to look for the "three Ws" when building a board: worker, wealth, wisdom. He had some great suggestions, and we were off and running. I was excited to build it overnight, but Hannah reminded me that it was a marathon, not a sprint. I didn't need to tackle it all right then, even though it was my subconscious way of getting *very busy*—so much so that I could not stop for too long to feel the pain of our loss. Working like this, I discovered, was an excellent coping strategy, until it damaged your body and disabled your ability to sleep.

I needed to find another, healthier way to manage the emotion of losing Alaina, and building the foundation—slow and steady, as Hannah was suggesting—was the key to its success. We slowly and methodically built the board to include a mental health specialist, a school administrator (with mental health background and knowledge), several business executives, an attorney, a leader from Bottlerock Napa Valley to guide our music vision, Hannah, and me. We have a really good mix, and while each brings one of the Ws to the board, everyone is connected to us in some meaningful way.

The most important aspect of the foundation was that all of us were in it together: working to advance the mission of being the positive change versus pointing the finger at what was wrong. Sure, we could have had an activist approach toward gun violence, but we were not haters. We were lovers. From day one. Our faith did not reward negativity. Instead, there was a levity to the culture we were building and a legacy we felt obligated to leave for Alaina. Any work we put into it was an act of service—and love for the dearest qualities of our daughter, which kept them in play.

It felt so good to watch Alaina's Voice Foundation take root and grow, keeping her spirit alive and her values relevant. Kindness was Alaina's way. Ask anyone who knew her; they would remember the gentle way she looked at them or how she spoke. I'll never forget my first botched attempt at teaching her about staring at others. Because the grocery store our family owned was located near a home for veterans, we received a fair number of customers who use wheelchairs. I didn't want our kids in the awkward position of seeing them for the first time without understanding how best to engage anyone who used a wheelchair. I felt a little bit like Homer Simpson as I laid down the law, "Alaina, if someone is different than you, you don't want to stare at them. Like if someone is in a wheelchair or if someone is really large or if they have different skin color. They might appear different, but we don't want them to feel treated differently." She stared up at me with her big hazel eyes and nodded as I continued my Oscar-worthy monologue, "Like if you see a person who is fat, you don't want to ask why they are fat or stare at them." Alaina looked startled. "Why daddy, is fat a bad word?"

I looked around the store, making sure nobody could hear me, aware this lesson was already long in the tooth and simply said, "Yes." Cringe. I know, right?

Alaina cocked her head, looked softly at me like she did, and nodded. "Okay."

Fast forward, Alaina was in preschool and had a great relationship with her teacher. One day when Alaina was not quite four years old, I picked her up. Her teacher had a quizzical look on her face, and with a slight grin, asked me if we could speak for a minute. I treaded softly past the other parents at pickup, wondering what she might have to share with me. Had Alaina had an "accident"? Had she done something that threw the teacher or another student off? I had no clue. I was relieved to hear her preface our conversation when we stepped into the other room. "I have a funny story for you. I was speaking to one of the other teachers about this diet shake I had been drinking, and I told her it had no fat. Not long after I see Alaina staring at me in angst. I said, 'Alaina, sweetie, what is wrong?' Alaina replied, 'You said a bad word!'"

My eyebrows were raised as I matched the teacher's grin. She then told me, "I thought, *Oh shit, what did I say?* I leaned over and said, 'Alaina, it's okay. You can tell me the word, so I know.' Alaina replied, 'You said fat.'"

I shook my head, feeling my chest about to explode with laughter. The teacher was so relieved but couldn't stop smiling and we laughed over Alaina's innocence and sincerity. I told her about my lesson in staring, and it gave us both a chuckle about how the way we teach can sometimes backfire. I realized I was probably a bit premature on this lesson.

No matter what, Alaina developed a sensitivity for others, especially those who were different from her. She carried that for the next fourteen years, buying into my well-intentioned debacle of a lesson. After her death, we receive a lot of stories about Alaina's interaction with acquaintances and strangers, whom she never put second to her close friends. Everyone in front of Alaina had value, and while she had learned not to stare at what made people different, she saw them, and they felt honored by her presence. She was literally embodying the positive change.

One day, I received a call from a girl who also went to Pepperdine and wanted to share a story about Alaina. When she met Alaina, she had recently lost her brother to a skateboarding accident and told me, "I was also a freshman at Pepperdine about a week before the shooting. I was feeling down and sitting at the Starbucks on campus when Alaina literally just plopped down in the seat next to me and said, "Hi, I'm Alaina, what's your name?" It was such a kind gesture when I needed it, and we were instant friends."

These were the stories that gave us goosebumps, that buoyed our mission with the foundation, encouraged us to grow it, preserve, and yes, promote Alaina's kindness. One day we learned another story about a friend of Alaina's from high school who had been struggling on campus. Apparently, Alaina had gone out of her way to make him feel welcome with her friend group and they all became so close. Her outgoing personality and kindness made it happen. She lived with an open heart. She listened with an open mind. Her eyes saw goodness and mitigated differences. How she navigated the world at that young age showed she was born to radiate love, to teach it in the way she spoke, acted, and interacted. We would continue to hear story after story of similar friendliness and acts of kindness that made people feel better.

Her roommate from Pepperdine, Lauren, shared one particular story about Alaina's capacity to study and watch a show at the same time. "I don't know how she would do it. We were all studying for great books (a first-year Socratic seminar centered on classic texts), which is a lot of reading. Somehow Alaina would be watching another episode of *Friends* while reading but still be 100 percent involved in the conversation of the suite as if nothing else was happening. All the while she would totally absorb the reading." That was our Alaina. She never wanted to miss out on anything, so she had mastered multitasking. She loved school and prioritized her studies, so it was easy for us to focus on education as one of the aspects of the foundation. Alaina's Voice provides scholarships to the high school graduates of Napa's local schools, to keep them on their path toward getting an education.

Alaina's Voice Foundation (AVF) has also helped fund a webcast about an astronaut who was a local Vintage High School graduate, only one of two women at the international space station from Northern California (one from Petaluma and one from Vintage High School). We wanted to show the youth of our valley, and even more so, our girls, that they can do anything they set their mind to. The webcast, live from the space station, was initially shown at Vintage High School, but we soon made it available to all schools in Napa Valley.

Music had always been a passion of Alaina's, so it was easy for us to fold that into the foundation too. To perpetuate her love of singing, we hosted a captivating concert with the humanitarian rock musician, Michael Franti, whose messages of hope, love, kindness, and positivity spoke to Alaina's soul and the foundation's central themes. He invited kids on stage to dance and had recently released a song about gun violence called "Flower and the Gun," which coincidentally happened to be recorded *just before* the Borderline shooting. His production team tried to get us into the music video, but it was a little too late and released a few weeks later.

We could not have had a more perfect event to launch the foundation. Michael energized the entire organization, got us up and moving, and helped release some calcified grief with his uplifting songs. With the help of our board member, Dave Graham, Alaina's Voice Foundation was able to take off with this community event. While we were blessed by Graham's access to Franti, we soon discovered that getting bigger names costs more money, but we were able to have our second concert a few years later in 2021 with Matt Nathanson. Just as we emerged from Covid, Nathanson put on a great show and turned out to be a hilarious storyteller. Attendance was lower than we had hoped as California had dropped the newest mask mandate only days before, which limited our attendance. Even so, we sold more than 1,800 tickets and had a great time. Since then, we learned that while we love music venues, the cost far exceeds the foundation's capacity, and we have to remind ourselves of its mission: not necessarily to entertain but to uplift by being the positive change. We can do that without a big-name musician, though it sure is fun to host one and share the kind of good vibes that only music provides. The point is that everyone desperately wanted and needed music for their own soul during Covid and we felt good that we could restore a little bit of the joy that so many had lost during the pandemic. With so much despair and bewilderment, music was a potent medicine to heal us all.

While music helped restore our mental state, we were well aware of the spike in suicides during the pandemic when social distancing took its toll on everyone. Humans need each other. Social isolation was doing nothing to support that need. While music events might pull us out of our hibernation, we knew mental health needed attention. We quickly learned about the shortage of access to therapists. After Covid, every therapist was already caught on umpteen video calls assisting everyone else. The need to talk to someone, *anyone* with a degree in clinical therapy was very hard to fulfill and we wanted to do something about it.

One evening, I was scrolling through Facebook and read a very disturbing message from a vet who sounded suicidal. I knew the person but not that well. Sensing he might need help, I sent him a private message and suggested he call the mental health specialist on our board. Luckily, we got to him when we did. He's in a much better place now and really wants to help support other veterans like himself. This was the beginning of our pathway for the Bridge Therapy Services through AVF.

Suicide soon became a real target for us. When a teen doesn't get access to a therapist after their third attempt at suicide, and the insurer can't provide for thirty days, we offer "bridge therapy" sessions. When a woman is beaten by her boyfriend in front of the children, both the mom and the children get the service provided. We are open to supporting the offender as well. The name of our services, Bridge Therapy, is about bridging the gap and getting people the support they need. That said, AVF doesn't replicate any services provided to our community by groups that are already doing their best work and have years of experience. For example, if an LGBTQ+ teen is contemplating suicide, we will refer them first to LGBTQ Connection where this is their specialty. Or if an abused woman seeks our help, we first look to Napa Emergency Women Services (NEWS). The list goes on with other great organizations in the Napa Valley that already support people in need.

One of the most exciting ventures we've taken on, in the spirit of Alaina's ability to listen closely to others, is a partnership with Teens Connect of the Mentis organization of Napa. With almost three decades of experience teaching high school, Hannah is acutely aware of the value of listening to what kids really need and want. By doing so, they reveal the future. She is a huge advocate for allowing kids to speak safely for themselves, rather than have parents or other adults tell them what they "should" want. All these initiatives have become the foundation of AVF and helped turn our grief into a purpose-driven pursuit of positive change in ourselves and our community.

Kindness Matters

PEOPLE OFTEN WANT to know what they can do to help another who is grieving. It's simple. Just be kind, we have no idea what is happening in others' lives. After navigating this loss for many years, I am well aware how the simplest act of kindness makes the biggest difference in another's life. One week after Alaina's murder, I walked into a Starbucks in North Napa near our home. I was desperately in need of an espresso jolt to keep going, yet when I went to pay, the young woman at the counter informed me my coffee was free. Someone in the room had bought it for me. I looked around. Who could it be?

Even though I felt vulnerable in that moment of receiving, I felt seen and comforted by the kindness of a stranger. Standing there, waiting for my coffee, the feeling of love was so palpable that I swear it filled the entire coffee shop. Even if nobody else knew about this transaction, they were all witnessing a powerful moment in my path toward healing.

    I continued to scan the room looking for someone who appeared that they might know me. No one was obvious, until I saw her. I had never met this woman before, yet she knew who I was. I made eye contact and knew it was definitely her. She walked toward me and quietly said, "I am so sorry for your loss. I saw the interview when you said, 'What if someone had just bought him a cup of coffee, would that have changed his day?'"

    I felt chills throughout my whole body, hearing my words on CBS come back to me. The timing of this small act of kindness really hit me in a way that made me want to do the same for others. The kind person who bought my coffee that day made me wonder about my own role in helping turn someone's day around. And what if one simple act of kindness could have changed the shooter's disposition? What if being kind could help someone reconsider being cruel? Was this act of kindness the catalyst to activate the fifth aspect of post-traumatic growth—helping me appreciate life? Did this stranger at Starbucks help me in my process? If so, I wondered if kindness is contagious. If it is, I wanted to start sharing it just like this woman did for me.

    Somehow, I was already tuning into the idea of spontaneous kindness. A simple act could go a long way in restoring someone's sense of worth and letting them know someone cares. Shortly after that day in Starbucks, I began to walk into a store or coffee shop and leave $5 or buy a large drink and, later, leave a teal rubber bracelet we created in Alaina's memory. The bracelets read "Kindness Matters" on one side and AlainasVoice.org on the other. Teal was Alaina's favorite color. They were a simple, perfect expression of her. Something to leave behind with the hope the message might stay forever, and the receiver would reciprocate.

Alaina was not new to spontaneous kindness. Kindness was at our daughter's core, and it inspired our family to follow. Years prior, Alaina's class was involved in delivering Christmas gifts to families in need, a tradition started by a dear friend Paige Dearden, who began adopting families from Community Outreach in Napa. After Paige's passing to breast cancer, a community of volunteers continued the delivery service in her honor. One year, I asked to participate with Alaina's class and was needed to translate for a Hispanic woman and her two-year-old daughter.

When we arrived at their home, I said in my best Spanish that we were there to bring food and gifts for her family. I stood at the threshold seeing minimal furniture and no gifts below the tiny Christmas tree. The mother was very gracious and allowed us to enter. As the procession of parent and student volunteers brought the bags and boxes of gifts and groceries through her door, she began to cry. I asked, "Why are you crying?" I thought she would be happy. She explained, "Last night my husband was in tears. He's working two jobs to try and help with all the bills, and for the second year, he couldn't afford to buy any of us Christmas gifts." The woman was going through some major medical issues, and all their money was going to pay what they could while also paying other bills. She continued, "He will be so happy we can't thank you enough."

I stood there taking all this in, fighting off the tears. It felt so good to help this family.

After helping Paige and the Vichy Elementary team of volunteers do this for a few years, I decided to adopt a family with Hannah, Alaina, Alex, and anyone on our grocery store staff who wanted to help too. Our adopted family was a Hispanic couple in their sixties and their two twenty-something autistic sons. The mother, Rosa, had the greatest challenge caring for her son Jose, who was in a wheelchair with severe autism and an extreme stomach issue which required all his food to be liquified. Rosa was very kind and humble, expressing her gratitude when we delivered our gifts and food. She couldn't stop thanking us, and it struck me that she would be fighting this fight all year long, not just at Christmas. Jose was scheduled for another major stomach surgery soon. I told Rosa and the social worker that she was welcome to come into my Ranch Market Napa store anytime to get any groceries she needed, and that we would pay for all of it. She was in tears and extremely grateful. Shortly after that day, I started to receive text messages from Rosa, which nearly always lead with the word *bendiciones*, which means blessings in Spanish. She was also very devoted to her faith.

A couple months later, the social worker called to ask if she could bring Rosa to the store for groceries. I reiterated the invitation—Rosa was welcome anytime and could have whatever she needed to support her sons and husband.

The social worker informed me that Rosa had only come one time prior and refused to take more than rice and dried beans. I was shocked, assuming she would have gone on a shopping spree, but Rosa took only what she needed. Her understanding of taking just enough was humbling. She was grateful for every bean and grain of rice, taking nothing more, asking for nothing else. Her humility and graciousness were indelible. I had never met a more selfless person. Knowing that she would never give herself more than rice and beans, we managed to sneak in chicken, vegetables, and more in her bags. She did not reject this, and we were happy. Sadly, Jose passed after his long battle with his ailments, but Rosa texted another *bendiciones* and a picture of Jose smiling.

Fast forward two years later. Approximately two weeks after Alaina's murder, I received another message from Rosa, with a picture of Jose with angel wings. Again, she wrote *bendiciones* and added, "Jose will look after Alaina in heaven." I was extremely touched. I did not expect to hear from her but when I did, my heart broke open, feeling her compassion and love. It was just the beginning of the season of spontaneous kindness that would buoy us in the midst of our despair.

Acts of kindness, we were learning, were like the pavers we could step upon to find our way forward. One simple act followed by another, and another, would lead us to a higher resonance someday.

Three years later, after practicing spontaneous kindness, I received a reference to another family in Napa who had transitioned from homelessness into their own place, but they had hardly anything. After speaking to the oldest son who was 18, I learned that in addition to his single mom, he had a younger brother who was nine years old. They had one mattress, two pillows, a bath towel, and a few other things they had acquired from friends. Hannah and I discussed this. It was around Christmas time, and we needed so little, so we agreed to support this family instead. We reached out to our friend Mike to see if he and his wife wanted to combine resources. They agreed and met us at Target to offer this mother and her two sons a shopping spree.

When we arrived at Target, the mother was so grateful. She didn't understand what was happening. The oldest son translated in Spanish, until he realized that both Mike and I could speak it. Although Mike was more proficient in his Spanish, we both managed to keep suggesting more items to the mom. She couldn't believe it—first that we were trying to communicate in her native language but more so, that we were encouraging her to fill her cart. She selected a toaster but asked to put it back so that she could get a coffee maker instead.

She looked at us, "I don't drink alcohol but is it okay for coffee? I can put the toaster back."

We all looked at each other and stood there in disbelief. Mike's wife broke the awkward silence and insisted she get both. The mom looked pleased yet startled, trying to contain her surprised smile. We continued to encourage her to get whatever she needed for her household. And so it went. In the meantime, while our wives were helping the mom choose kitchen supplies, we headed to clothing and bedding to get some gifts for the boys. The younger son stayed home because we wanted the gifts for him to be more of a surprise, allowing us to play Santa Claus. Off we went with the older son to get gifts, socks, underwear, and clothes for his nine-year-old brother. When it came time for the oldest son to get some stuff for himself, we quickly realized none of the clothes reflected his feminine sense of style. All along, it was evident that the oldest son was LGBTQ+ which I was not sure how Mike, an old white guy, would take. When Mike came over to see how he was making progress, the boy said, "I make some of my own clothes and I like things that are more feminine looking." I drew in a deep breath praying that this amazing moment would not go sideways. My palms were sweating, standing there in the aisle between them, not knowing which way this would go. Mike and I had never discussed these things, and while I knew our family was open and supportive of the LGBTQ+ community, we did not know how Mike's family felt.

My heart was pounding in that pregnant pause after the son had revealed himself. And what happened next blew me away. Mike drew in a frustrated breath, "Well shit, why didn't you say something? We've been wasting our time over here." Mike promptly led us over to the women's section and to my astonishment, began to hold up women's sweaters and pants to himself to see if the oldest son liked the style. The teenager looked at me and grinned. I nodded. Who knew? Nothing was said. We just continued the shopping spree. It's amazing how humanity works when we allow each other to be who we were. It felt simple. It felt right. Being kind to each other. Being what we are all capable of being to rise above the petty differences that divide us and draw us into darkness. Again, I wondered about the shooter and other perpetrators. Had anyone ever reached out to help them? Would it have changed our family's story? All these things flashed through my mind while Mike held up women's clothes in front of the oldest son, as if he had done this with us millions of times. I wondered what our world might look like if this became our new normal.

In the meantime, I wandered back over to check on the moms, who were doing great work. The mother we were helping broke into tears, saying, "I don't understand why you are doing this." We said, "Someday you can help another, but today we are here for your family."

Supporting this single mother and her sons was an honor. We were so happy to have the opportunity to help this family and I admit, it felt great to play Santa Claus for a day. To this day, Mike and I can't enter Target without remembering what happened there and why. The metaphor was not lost on us either. Kindness is the target. Target kindness. Make it top of mind, the first thing you think about every single day. How can I be kind today? How can I serve? This approach to daily life was the antidote to my devastation and bewilderment, and while it would not bring our daughter back from the dead, it would make us more alive. Every time I do an act of kindness, I picture Alaina smiling down on me.

This act of service, of opening our hearts, was not only helping to rebuild our traumatized brains but also to become better people. More evolved. Less afraid. Ready and willing to grow, despite our pain, and finally one day outgrow it. Kindness is the cure for despair. When you have something outside pain that you want to reach, the pain diminishes and eventually dissolves. By focusing on this simple act of being kind, doing one act of spontaneous kindness daily, we were rising above the low vibrations of feeling victimized or losing our faith. Everyone has a choice. We chose to be kind, and it was significantly reshaping our world. Love, not hate, was driving us.

We have shared the story with our friends and others close to us. It is heartwarming to hear how other individuals and families have now taken up finding families to support in their times of need. I have a friend who continually buys Alaina's Voice bracelets so she can do something kind and then give others a bracelet. She told me that most times, she buys someone a Starbucks coffee and leaves the bracelet. Another friend makes cards with kind words and leaves them on a colleague's vehicle when she can tell they are having a bad day at work. I love hearing these stories. Kindness is enabling us to be creative.

Opportunities to be kind abound. One day, I was in downtown Napa and witnessed a young male in his early twenties riding his mountain bike down Main Street. Suddenly, someone inside a car opened the door to get out and the man on the bike slammed into the door. In cycling terms, the guy got "doored." Thankfully, he was uninjured, but his bike was mangled. He remained calm but frustrated trying to get to work at the Fatted Calf.

I walked over and offered to throw his bike in my truck and take him to work. He said yes and thanked me many times when I dropped him off. After I left, I drove straight to Walmart and bought a new bike and took it over to the rack outside his shop. I walked in and handed him the receipt.

"Take it back if you don't want it or use it as needed to get to work."

He looked at me quizzically. "Why are you buying me this bike?"

"You use this as your transportation to work, buy one for someone else someday."

He took a look at the new bike.

"You don't mind if I take it back, as I really liked my bike?"

I wanted to chuckle. Despite our best intentions and my need to be kind, I understood how others received my kindness was often very complicated and sometimes unexpected. Old Arik would have probably said, "You ungrateful asshole." Yet that was not me anymore.

I didn't mind at all that he asked; I actually thought it took some balls. It struck me that if he was riding to work, he probably did love his bike. I later realized that cyclists are connected to their bikes as if it is another body that becomes almost one with theirs. A swap and replace to get the job done isn't exactly the best outcome because of the sentimental value associated with most bikes in the cycling world. With a wiser voice, I was able to respond kindly to his request.

"I absolutely don't mind, and if you can use the money to get yours repaired, great."

"Thanks, man. Really. This is awesome. I don't know what to say other than thank you!"

I smiled and walked out, feeling good that I was there in the moment he needed help. Giving him a lift to work would have been enough, but having the resources to quickly resolve his next problem was something I wanted to give him to make his day easier. He thanked me, though I didn't even need or expect it. All I wanted was to give him a story that would remind him he was riding his bike one day and got doored, trashed his bike, and some guy gave him a ride and brought him a new bike. I wanted him to know humans can do humanity well sometimes. Most days, it's our inherent nature. And I hoped he would pass it forward.

Our culture, especially in the United States, is a tit for tat, score-keeping mentality. I do this for you, you do this for me. We often can't receive help because it makes us feel too vulnerable, as if we have lost our power, or worse, feel as though we are a burden to others. But what if allowing someone to be kind and allowing ourselves to receive kindness, we consequently return our humanity to each other? I can think of no better outcome for this practice. Being kind literally restores us to our innate nature, *human beings*, versus human doings. I'm not sure about you, but I was starting to like being more than doing. I was becoming a better human for it.

Always November

WITH ALL THE personal growth my family and I have experienced since 2018, we return every November to the anniversary of the shooting. It is an inescapable part of our process and an unavoidable combination of grief, sorrow and gratitude wrapped into one month. We really don't like referring to the shooting as an anniversary, yet it is the descriptor that fits. November is now such a mixed bag of emotions. While our favorite holiday as a family has always been Thanksgiving, November now comes with angst despite how much we have to be thankful for.

    To balance all of this and metabolize the emotions each year, Hannah and I have begun a ritual of going to the coast with our dog, Scout, a black lab who loves the water. We have always been dog people, and Hannah's favorite breed is the Labrador retriever. After having two chocolate labs, we got our first black lab, Scout, during the pandemic, and she has added so much to our life. She loves to swim and looks like a seal with her little black head bobbing above the waters near Sea Ranch, Jenner, or Bodega Bay where we've gone the last few years. The ocean is very comforting for us and helps us be present in the moment with each other. The coastal fog and rain during this time of year in Northern California lends another kind of peacefulness to our pilgrimage. Just hearing the rhythmic wash of waves breaking on the beach offers an inexplicable solace to our bond as a couple, and as individuals, when we are there.

During the four-year anniversary in 2022, we visited Sea Ranch when Scout was two years old. Having that kind of puppy energy buoyed us and we booked a dog-friendly Airbnb so that Scout could be with us for comfort and companionship. We were prepared for torrential rain, which was in the forecast, and surrendered to getting wet all weekend with Scout. However, the weather shifted on November 7th. Not only had the rain stopped but the sun was shining, and a beautiful rainbow filled the sky. Hannah and I could not help but smile, while Scout had a field day swimming in the river and along the coast. We did not need to talk to remember the day that Hannah drove through the rainbow after Alaina had passed. We deeply believed that Alaina was showing up that day to remind us that her light, brightness, and love were still with us.

We took great comfort in the gift of those perfect conditions to ease the pain of losing her, all over again during this anniversary. We paused many times just to listen to the crashing waves, to breathe it all in, together, while Scout ripped around the beach and ran in and out of the water. Scout's joy was palpable too and so potent. We had all the medicine we needed from the landscape to get through the anniversary and even enjoy it. The vision of the swells hitting the coastline and rocks reminded us of how tiny we were in our big world, and how huge our hearts could be when we felt our love for Alaina—and each other.

We loved our time at Sea Ranch, watching movies, working on puzzles, sipping comforting glasses of Chardonnay. We planned to cook and had every intention to do so. I love to cook and knew better than to rely on a vacation rental kitchen, so I packed up our SUV with all kinds of tools, spices, pots, knives, and anything else we needed to make some special meals. The point was to spend a lot of time together, to turn off our social media devices and just focus on each other. We made it a habit of turning off all our technology so that we could be together. It felt so heartwarming and unifying, and we didn't miss a thing on social media. The weekend brought us together, helped us slow down, reconnect and remind ourselves of the hard work we'd done to get this far in our healing.

It took years to process the pain of losing our daughter. I try to remind everyone who turns to me in their own grief that this is a process as precisely individual as each of us. There is no formula for getting over loss. There are, however, infinite ways to *get through it*. We continued to feel both grateful for what we had but also sad about what we had lost. This emotional equation will probably be a pattern for the rest of our lives.

To ease this particularly harsh reality of dipping back into the past, we found another ritual that we loved and looked forward to. We began stopping each year for lunch at Fishetarian just outside Bodega Bay for fish and chips. It gave us a chance to let Scout out of the car while we took a break and breathed it all in. Their snacks are great, so we always stock up and buy some fish before we hit the road. Devising a ritual like our trips to the coast each year was helping us build enough resilience to face the anniversary.

It seemed fitting to feel these waves of grief along the Pacific Coast. The emotional waves seemed significantly bigger the following year, 2023, on the fifth anniversary when Hannah suggested we try something new and visit Jenner—a tiny coastal town perched on a hill overlooking the Pacific. We were happy to get out of the car and take a long walk by the water with Scout, feeling grateful to have this time together, despite the forecast. Once again, the weather looked horrendous, however, we weren't going for the promise of sun but for peacefulness. Call it a coincidence, but somehow November 7, 2023, turned out to be beautiful, too, clear and sunny. I like to believe that Alaina was showing us that even in the darkness, there is light.

This cycle continued. Year after year. When it called for awful weather, we were greeted by sunshine, exquisite visibility, and rainbows. Our November ritual was having a dialogue with us, urging us to continue this tradition. Maybe it was because we had prioritized our peace and our presence with each other by turning off our phones. Just being together with Hannah felt like being on a long date with someone you love intimately and who knows your deepest vulnerabilities. We could turn to each other, in the silence of our sorrow and in the aliveness of our union, find peace—even with sixty pounds of black lab love in our laps.

Scout's happiness balanced the day and made each November 7th getaway something we could look forward to. This time seeing her play in the river and get so much joy from swimming and chasing ducks exponentially helped shift the focus away from our grief. Going away each year to honor the date—and reflect on what we had lost—and also on what we had *gained*—was the best decision we had ever made. We prioritized each other and restored our relationship. It felt even more powerful than our wedding anniversary. By turning off our phones, we had given all of ourselves to each other and the moment. We were painfully aware that we would never get this time back. It makes sense to always focus on the ones you love.

By year five, after dealing with grief for half a decade, we had built up so much resilience that we were better equipped to handle the swell. Still, it was the hardest anniversary for us to date. Perhaps it was because I was in the middle of writing this book and confronting some of the pain in these pages. Perhaps it was just timing. Things felt more emotional than usual leading up to the five-year anniversary, but I remembered grief was like a beach ball and was able to allow it to surface when it needed to from time to time.

I was getting better at sensing when it might pop up again and had grown more skilled at handling the pain. But this year I was feeling particularly anxious, not just because of the hole I still felt in my heart for the infinite ways I still missed Alaina. Every. Single. Day. Something else was also gnawing away at me.

For a while, I had been feeling disheartened with the actions of many of the employees in my family business that I had owned and been operating for 27 years. I had lent money, given time, and supported some individuals like family only to be met with theft or lies. I was sitting with the pain of giving so much in friendship and feeling betrayed. As I sat there, listening to the ocean next to the Jenner Inn, I was feeling the toll of running the business and considering what I should do about it when my phone buzzed with a text alert. It was a friend, Jose. The text read:

> *Hello Arik,*
> *I just made a delivery to your store in Napa. Will you be needing a special order again? Please let me know. And on another note: This may be a subject for a personal conversation, but to make the story short, my wife and I used to own a market back in Maryland. We had the best time working there, but something happened, and we felt it was best to sell and move to the area. And ever since I've been hoping for an opportunity to become a store owner again. So, I just wanted to mention if you ever decide to sell one of your stores please consider us, we would love to buy it from you. And please forgive me if this is a bit strange.*

But they say, "If you don't ask, you will never know, right!"
Thank you for listening.
Jose

I read it again and felt something shift in me—a tilt toward a new chapter of life. I had not considered selling the business, which had been in our family since my parents started the stores in the early seventies. My brother had his own businesses. Alex was in England with dreams of becoming a professional soccer player and Alaina was not around to weigh in on what she wanted to do with the rest of her life, which we all knew would not have been to run the grocery stores. I wondered if on the five-year anniversary of her death, she wanted me to take a good look at my future and bring more ease to her parents' days.

I picked up my phone and texted Jose: *I am away for a couple days but will reach out when I am back.* I sat there for a moment, watching the waves break beneath the Jenner Inn, aware that something was urging me to consider what I would be doing next. It might have been hard for me to accept this nudge from the universe, but I sensed I was being prepared to do something more fulfilling. My gut carried this instinct, but I couldn't yet reconcile it. I wondered, too, if this was God's way of giving me a kick in the butt to move forward with my grief journey.

Later that day, I told Hannah. We discussed the proposition but decided to wait until the time felt right. However, I couldn't deny a suspicion that our daughter was up to her loving ways—urging me to keep letting go to grow. Was she really guiding me to let go of the family store? Wow. This would be pivotal. I was still uncertain, but sitting there, working on the book in Jenner, I had that gut check knowing that Alaina was once again still with us.

Fast forward to the end of the month when we turned our focus on love and gratitude at Thanksgiving. That year, we had the blessing of hosting our dear friend, Jeneen, Alaina's spiritual godmother. Jeneen' first trip to join our family for Thanksgiving was 2018, when she was asked to escort Alaina home from her first semester at Pepperdine. She never got to fulfill her role, but we all decided she should still come up for Thanksgiving that year. She humbly accepted and has continued the tradition ever since. We love spending time with her and all the discussions we get to share. It's easy with her; we don't feel we need to entertain her. She is just absorbed into the flow, like family, and all is well. She is also fun to binge-watch TV series with because she chooses not to have a paid service provider. She also gets along well with our extended British family, Mark and Sarah, who also share in our annual Thanksgiving prep and celebration. The girls make pies and bake for a couple of days. I map out the game plan for the turkey and the logistics in the kitchen, Mark makes roasted potatoes, and Alex says he will bake the "stuffin muffins" (stuffing baked like a savory muffin) that he sometimes makes. We love just being together. At the same time, it is always difficult, of course.

We cannot deny that our daughter is missing from the kitchen and the Thanksgiving table. Hannah always makes two chocolate pies. Being chocolate lovers, she and Alaina baked them every year, so we continue the tradition. We add more pies to the spread: apple, pumpkin and pecan. Nobody needs that many pies, but continuing these traditions keeps Alaina with us, in spirit, and the memories and stories alive. Equally hard, however, is navigating Alex's absence while he has been in England studying over Thanksgiving. While neither of our children could join us these past few holidays, we feel their love and we are grateful for the time we were given with Alaina and for the time we still get with Alex.

After the holidays, it felt right to move forward with Jose's inquiry about selling the store. He was right. If we don't ask, nothing happens in life. He had taken the first step in reaching out to us and he seemed to have genuine motivations and experience. For months I weighed all the possibilities. Alaina was clearly guiding me to let go of what had been a major focus for most of my career. Seven months later, after a ton of family discussions, we closed the deal.

To my surprise, instead of feeling anxious, we felt liberated but also equally sad. We shared so many memories, both good and not so good, but the store had stitched our community together and it suddenly wasn't mine to manage any more. However, Alaina's plan had been accomplished. She had freed me to move on to the next thing. To finish this book. To speak. To help others through their grief and to remind them to build their reservoir of resilience. And so, I carried my stories with me into this wonderful new beginning.

In the summer of 2024, we sold our flagship store. The feeling of selling something that had been such a huge piece of our lives for forty-eight years brought much emotion. Some businesspeople might look at the final deal and think the details weren't standard, yet it felt right. The new owner had past experience owning a store. His family wanted to keep the name, which meant a lot to me to keep my parents' legacy going. He wanted to work in the store as a family, like we did when we were young. The trust that was immediately apparent between the new owner and me just felt right. Ironically, every time we have a conversation, we discover we have more in common. While I know he never knew Alaina, every time I walk in the store he is wearing an Alaina's Voice bracelet. The irony is not lost on me. In losing our daughter, I had cultivated more trust in life, not less. I had created more relationships and found new friends. I had opened up my mind, shifted my thoughts and what I believed was possible—beyond anything I could have conceived prior to Alaina's death. I realize this is not the case with so many people who have faced similar gut-wrenching and unthinkable situations. My heart had opened to life and stayed warm—not cold. My broken-open heart was not bitter but beautifully expansive. Developing resilience had enabled me to keep loving life no matter what it presented. I now know that if I pay attention to the signs, everything aligns eventually.

The week after the sale was finalized, I stopped by Alaina's gravesite. It had been a while since my last visit. Oddly, I'd never felt deeply connected to her there. Graves are markers, but the soul feels elusive. Yet, I stood there, surrounded by the soft rustling of trees and the quiet hum of the world moving on. I found peace in the stillness and a kind of silent recognition that I was there to honor her spirit, acknowledging a truth I had long carried with me.

A month earlier, I sat across from a friend, a father, who had just lost his child to cancer. He wore the weight of it on his face, in the way his hands fidgeted with the coffee cup, trying to find something to hold onto. I knew that weight. I knew the helplessness he felt, the unanswerable question of why we can't save the ones we love from suffering.

He spoke, his voice soft but heavy with grief. I listened, seeing the pain in his eyes, understanding that no words could offer the comfort he sought. All I could do was witness his sorrow and let him know I was there, as someone who understands. Grief has many faces. Our losses are not the same, but the ache beneath them is shared.

As I stood at Alaina's gravesite, I realized the grief never leaves us. It simply changes shape. It lingers in unexpected moments, in conversations with friends over breakfast, in the quiet reflection of a visit to the past. The heart keeps score of its scars, but with each beat, we keep going. We keep living, despite our losses. There, in the quiet, I made peace with that truth.

It wasn't my job to save Alaina. As her father, I was here to love her—every day, not just on the anniversary of her passing. November will always carry something life-changing for me, a reminder to "Let go and Let God." These days, I no longer worry about control; I am simply present—and that is enough. Many still wonder how I can find gratitude after enduring so much heartache and loss. But I have learned that, even in sorrow, there is still love, hope, kindness, and a quiet sense of gratitude. No matter the day, the week, or the month, it is always November.

Questions We are Asked

ALAINA'S PASSING GAVE me the opportunity to become an expert in resilience and grief. Over the years, many people began turning to me, seeking guidance and a path forward through their own grief. I have discovered that when I speak to groups nowadays, many people share the same questions, which I've shared below. I've also asked my son, Alex, to share his thoughts. Some of the questions I have been asked I answer. Some of them, we both answer, and some questions Alex was asked he put in his responses. Neither of us have a background in counseling, but we offer a perspective through our lived experience and hope it might help you or a friend chart your own journey toward healing.

How do you do it? (i.e., what they mean is how can you keep living after losing so much?)

We were blessed with 18 years of Alaina's life. Many others are not so fortunate. We lived, laughed, and loved as a family. We have so many amazing memories. Don't get me wrong, it really truly sucks. It is painful, emotional, and leaves a true emptiness, but if you gave me a choice of the years I had with Alaina or eternity with another, I will always choose Alaina.

You are a man of faith. Do you ever sit and wonder why God let this tragedy happen?

We do our best not to go down what we call the "Dark Road of Why." We don't know many details about the man who took Alaina and eleven other lives that night. Many of the families chose to find out all the details. While there was a temptation to want to know more, that dark road called why doesn't change the fact that Alaina is no longer with us in body. A few of the family members have voiced regret for finding out the details. I assume it would haunt me, too.

Can you avoid grief?

No. Grief is unavoidable. At some time in our lives we will experience grief, in the loss of a loved one, a pet, the dream job, or a relationship. It's all grief, and it is different for each and every one of us. Grief has less power over us when we respect it as a powerful change agent.

Is there a right way to do grief?

No. There is no right or wrong way to do grief, it's just grief. Some cry, some are angry, some don't want to speak about it. Each of our stories determines how we respond. It's a process and each person will have their own unique experience.

How is your son handling it?

Alex is amazing and resilient. He has humor, kindness, strength, character, and focus. After the mass shooting in Uvalde and Buffalo, Alex turned to me and said, "Dad, how can I reach out to those families?" I replied, "Why, bud?" He said, "I am sure there are siblings who just lost someone, I would be willing to speak to them if they want to not feel alone."

Do you remember that night?

(*Alex*) I don't think anyone has heard my side of the story. To be honest, I don't think I have shared it nor do I like to reflect or think back on it.

I was woken up early, I don't even remember what time, but it was early. The first thing I see are my parents crying and my dad says, "There has been an accident with your sister." Then they hug me and my mom prays. I walk down the hall and see Lorrie and Dave there and Lorrie hugs me too. I wasn't aware of what was going on, so I didn't really cry when my parents told me, I was emotional, but I thought she was probably okay. Next thing I know I am packing a bag and we're on our way to the airport. I remember stopping at a gas station and the first person who texted me was Aidan Cushing, I just remember saying it's okay and he responded with, it's not okay. And that hit me truly, I didn't really know what to say, but it just resonated with me.

I remember getting on the plane and being in the front row which was pretty nice. Before the plane took off, I texted Alaina saying something along the lines of, "Are you okay? Please tell me you're okay, please text back." Then we took off and I just kept watching my parents the whole day and observing their emotions and seeing them and how they held onto each other the whole day. They would always cling onto me, but I just remember my mom crying on my dad's shoulder and my dad being emotional on the flight too.

When we landed my uncle picked us up and we headed straight to the information center. He had been texting and calling hospitals but none of them had Alaina. But he was doing so much for us and when he heard the news that night, he was in LA already making calls and driving all over. It all honestly felt like a simulation, time was moving slowly, and it felt as though everything was clouded and melancholy. We arrive at the information center and the first thing that happens is a camera is stuck right into my uncle's face from some news channel. Just this lack of privacy and consideration for my uncle but at the time I didn't think anything of it, I kind of thought it was cool that I may be on TV.

Next thing you know we're walking into the building, past a bunch of people who are also crying and sad, and then we get led to this room with a few people in it. The only people I knew were Chris and Amy and then my uncle of course.

Eventually, someone walks in, the guy sits down and says a few things and then says sorry, and my parents break into tears. I don't even think he said sorry for your loss, it was just sorry, and they already knew. I was sitting next to my parents as they embraced each other but I was emotionless. I didn't know what to do, I was in shock. Then my parents embraced me too and the main thing I remember one of the people saying is, "Tell stories, that is what will help with the grief."

The rest of the day we spent in the house of the vice chancellor of Pepperdine, it was kind of creepy, to be honest, and we were embraced with love from all our friends and family. I remember getting toys from one of the local toy shops in Malibu. Just everything that everyone did for us as a family during the tragedy and after was amazing. The constant love and support we received was what helped us get through the loss. I want to say thank you to every single one of those people that helped us and that was there for us when we needed them.

There was one thing I remember going through my head that day, "why?" Why Alaina? Why not someone else? Why our family? I remember praying to God and asking why did you take Alaina away from us. I look back on those questions with regret. I wouldn't want what happened to us, what happened to Alaina, to happen to anyone else. It's a horrible feeling and I understand why I asked why. I was lost, upset, and sad, I knew I would never get to see my sister again. I would think about all the times we could have had together and how I wouldn't get to be an uncle. But now

I have had time to reflect and grow up and look back over five years ago. Everything happens for a reason. I wouldn't be where I am today without my sister and without what happened. I knew from that day on that I needed to be there and be strong for my parents. It helped me grow up and Alaina is one of my biggest motivators. I love her and miss her, and I will forever be grateful for the time we had together on this Earth. I know she is watching over my family and me and one day I will join her, and we will all be together as a family again.

I am afraid to let my loved ones go in fear something will happen, how do you do it?

(*Arik*) You have to trust life. You have to let people live their lives without trying to overprotect them. Living a fear-based life is a limited one. Choose the most expansive life you can. You only get one chance at this life. Choose trust. Choose to find joy in the midst of your despair.

Did you and your sister get along?

(*Alex*) Yes and no. I mean, it was the usual case of a big sister and an annoying little brother. I would always antagonize and make her mad because I found it fun. That was until she hit me or took something that belonged to me. The funniest was when I would eat her food in the fridge, which she did not label by the way, and then she would scold me for eating her food which I didn't know was hers. Or when I would say that I was humble and then she would say, "you're not humble if you say you're humble." That one was always funny too, so I continued to say that I was humble since she would always respond with that line in a "teaching" tone. That's why I would call her my second mom because she would always get after me, but she was always caring too. Whenever I needed help with schoolwork she would always be there to help. If I was ever down or sad she would check in on me. We would also talk smack about our parents after we would get in trouble or one of us got in trouble. She would ask about what was going on in school and if anything was going on with my friends. We would bond over random stuff too like TV shows in specific. We always would have our moments, but we did get along and I'm grateful for all the time that I had with my sister.

Do your son and wife know how you speak so highly of them?

(*Arik*) Alex gives Hannah and me so much strength. We definitely try to tell him and have, yet we also don't want to overwhelm him with it too much. I have told Hannah many times how she gives me strength and I can't imagine doing this without her. That said, try to tell the people you love how much they mean to you and sometimes even be courageous enough to get super specific.

(*Alex*) No. I'm so used to my dad making fun of me all the time that I never knew he spoke so highly of me—kidding. On a real note, I genuinely did not. My Mom and Dad have always told me how proud they are of me, and it means a lot because one of the things I always try to do is to make my parents proud. They have done so much for me that saying thank you will never be enough. I feel this need to repay them—in a good way—by making them proud, by making the most of everything I do, and by working hard.

How could you let Alex go so far to college?

(*Arik*) Alex chose his path, as did Alaina. I don't believe we should tell them where to go. It is our job to build their character. If I had pushed Alaina to go to Pepperdine and the outcome still happened, could I live with myself? I don't know the answer. So, when it came time for Alex to choose his college, he wanted to give soccer a shot. He works hard and had above a 4.6 GPA. Who was I to tell him no? It is hard to have him living so far away, but we love that he is enjoying his experience. And that is what his life is, his experience. It is not my job to put a bubble around my son in fear something could happen. Because let's be honest, something could happen. It happened to Alaina, and she was much closer to home in the "safest city in America."

(*Alex*) Football/soccer is why. Football is something that I love and enjoy playing and I'm trying to make it to the next level. Being here allows me to get my education and pursue my dreams simultaneously while being enveloped in a completely different culture. A culture where I will bike past a pub at 11 a.m. and see two lads having a pint, then bike past again at 7 p.m. and there they are with another pint.

Of course, I miss home and the weather and the food and my family and my dog. But it has been a good experience for me so far. It is very far. I spend six months away from home and it's over a day of travel to get home. So, I do get homesick, but honestly, God has been a big help for me being so far away from my family. To be honest, my faith didn't grow too much after my sister passed, it was being on my own and being so far away from my family that helped me build my faith. I remember being here and crying the first night, but then I prayed and asked for strength and support from God. From then on, I have been growing my faith and my relationship with God which has helped me to deal with being so far away.

How do you feel about guns?

(*Arik*) I am a gun owner. It doesn't take a gun to kill people. It takes hate. Timothy McVeigh didn't need a gun to blow up the Oklahoma Federal building killing over 250 people. At the same time, should we be handing them out so freely over the counter to anyone walking up? What if there has been a recent domestic dispute between a husband and wife, how do you think she would feel if she heard her husband recently purchased a gun? Safe? I think not. Politicians need to stop worrying about who might not vote for them and do what is right when no one is looking. Owning a gun is a right, as well as a privilege. I believe over ninety percent of gun owners support background checks and wait periods. Many states don't require that to happen. Again, I have zero problem with people owning guns, because let's be honest, they aren't going away, that is not real. However, can we have a system to make sure an 18-year-old on his birthday has a check to make sure he's not suicidal or hasn't posted on his Instagram that he wants to go into a school or somewhere and shoot people. A check is essential. Before anyone can drive, we must get a permit, because anyone can kill someone if they are unsafe behind the wheel. The same applies to gun ownership. Get checked first, get the permit, then get the gun. This seems like a no-brainer and the data backs this up as the surest way to keep our communities safe.

(*Alex*) I don't see the problem with having guns for hunting, maybe having a handgun for self-defense or protection. It's having an AR-15, an AK-47, etc. that I feel is wrong. The Second Amendment is out of date. The amendment was created when our country was small, to have a militia when necessary. The country pours plenty of money into our military these days, so there is no need for a militia ever to be required again. The other point is access to guns. It's too easy for people to get a gun of any sort in this country. Background checks and these behind-the-scenes actions will help for sure. Yes, there will still be people bringing guns into the country or always finding the back door to get a gun, but the background checks at least make it a bit harder for people to acquire a gun. So, I don't mind guns. I understand why some people have them for hunting or protection. It's the heavy firearms that are unnecessary and how easy it is for someone to get a gun that I feel is wrong.

Does it hurt when you hear about another mass shooting?

(*Arik*) Yes, every single time it crosses my mind to get on a plane or in a car and go to the place. Deep down, I want to be there for these people to let them know, sadly, they are not alone. At this point, I wish it was just me and my family, but it is not and there are more joining my painful club every year. It really is time for our country's leaders to have a conversation about what is real. A conversation of protecting our people while still allowing our rights. We need both sides of the aisle to step to the middle. There is no silver bullet to fix this issue—no pun intended. It will take creativity and real conversations, not the current scenario which includes earplugs and a bullhorn.

(*Alex*) It truly does. Every time I hear of a mass shooting it makes me sad. It makes me feel that I am not the only one that went through losing someone to a mass shooting, but that's horrible. Too many people have been affected by mass shootings and gun violence in general and it seems like this "club" is just growing at an exponential rate. I don't want anyone to experience what we have or lose someone to a mass shooting. The saddest thing is mass shootings are so common nowadays that when you hear about one in the news, even for me, it's not even a surprise anymore. I pray that something will change in the U.S. but deep down I know that change won't happen for a while.

How do you get up every day?

(*Arik*) Hannah is my rock. She said to me, not long after losing Alaina, maybe even that same morning. "We have a son who does not deserve to live in the shadow of his dead sister." That echoes in my mind all the time, we live for him and for each other. I still try to think of things Alaina did every day that make me smile. She was a gift. The second piece, our communities stood behind us in full force. From family friends to people we didn't know, from Napa to Thousand Oaks to Pepperdine, in the end we were surrounded with so much love, hope and faith, it is the least we can do to give that back to those around us.

When you say you encouraged her to go out that night, do you regret it?

(*Arik*) No, we believe she was in the right place at the right time when evil walked in. She was a college student; she was doing nothing wrong. She was living her life, experiencing the world. It was not our job to keep her locked inside her door room or at the library. Nobody knew what was about to happen at Borderline that night, just as nobody knows what will happen from the minute they walk out their door each day. Life is random. We accept that. At the same time, we wish it was different. We wish we could hug her again. We wish we could see her smile or feel her kindness, yet we can if we just try to remember. It is not easy, but we definitely can still feel her with us.

I can't sleep after my loss. How do you sleep?

(*Arik*) I try to just breathe and remember the good times. I miss Alaina immensely. This is my beach ball, but it's not too heavy. It sucks to have the beach ball of grief, but I can handle it. I have learned to just breathe. It takes time. For years, I would wake up at 12:36 a.m., the time we received the phone call. As time went on, I would wake up at other points like 1:30, 2:30, 3:30 in the morning, but after a year this pattern stopped on its own. I didn't have to control my grief or force my recovery. I just had to allow for it over time. As the saying goes, time heals.

How do you stay so positive?

(*Arik*) We don't know why we immediately found acceptance. We didn't seem to go through the stages of grief. Cultivating positivity is a choice, but we are pretty convinced our experience was more of post-traumatic growth. We feel so blessed to have had the time we did. Don't get me wrong, it is still very hard. Off and on, Hannah and I will just give each other a look and one or both of us will tear up. We are filled with so much joy and so much sorrow simultaneously.

This must be so hard. How do you function?

(*Arik*) For each of us, our life and our journey is like a fingerprint. Similar from afar but very different. Even for Alex, Hannah, and me, we have been through a similar loss yet have experienced it in different ways. There is no perfect way to do grief, yet the emotion is the love and the loss.

Does it seem healing for you to speak and/or write about your story?

(*Arik*) No. It is not healing for me, but it definitely is fulfilling to help others in their darkest times. If I can help someone when they don't feel they can survive to feel less alone, that is important. As for healing completely, I am not sure there will ever be an end point to this journey. I'm just being honest. I wish I could say there is a definite moment when it all stops hurting. That is not real. It still hurts. A lot. I miss Alaina each and every day, but I do my best to think of things that make me smile about her to help when the waves of sorrow hit.

What is post-traumatic growth?

(*Arik*) Post-traumatic growth (PTG) is the positive psychological change that can occur in the aftermath of a traumatic event. It is a concept that has gained increasing attention in recent years as researchers and mental health professionals have sought to understand the ways in which individuals can not only recover from trauma but also emerge stronger and more resilient. PTG is a process that involves significant personal growth and positive transformation in the face of adversity. It can involve changes in one's worldview, values, relationships, and sense of personal identity. These changes can manifest in a number of ways, including increased compassion, a greater appreciation for life, improved relationships, and a sense of purpose or meaning.

While PTG may not occur in every individual who experiences a traumatic event, it has been observed across a range of traumatic experiences, from serious illness to combat, natural disasters, and in our case, the loss of a loved one from a mass shooting incident. PTG is not a denial of the negative aspects of trauma, but rather a recognition of the potential for growth and positive change in the aftermath of adversity.

The concept of PTG has important implications for the treatment of trauma, as it highlights the potential for individuals to not only recover but to thrive in the wake of traumatic events. Mental health professionals may use techniques such as cognitive behavioral therapy, narrative therapy, and mindfulness-based interventions to facilitate post-traumatic growth. By helping individuals to reframe their experiences and find new meaning in their lives, these interventions can help to facilitate the growth and positive transformation that is characteristic of PTG. It seems synchronistic that when we sat down as a family to Voice Foundation, Be the Positive Change was established almost immediately.

What is a grief partner?

(*Arik*) Someone you can confide in when you're navigating the waters of grief. It's best not to do this alone, in my opinion. Having someone to trust and confide in relieves such a huge weight. Truly allowing those times of vulnerability and being able to be open with your grief partner is such a blessing and honor. While it is a large undertaking, if someone finds themselves looking to you in their anxiety or fear of how hard it is, please know, there is no greater honor than to help them.

Acknowledgments

THIS BOOK WOULD never have come to life without the unwavering love and support of so many.

First, to my wife and soulmate, Hannah—I couldn't imagine this journey without you. You've propped me up in my darkest hours, and you've allowed me the gift of doing the same for you. Your patience and encouragement throughout the writing process have been nothing short of extraordinary. I am endlessly grateful.

To Alex — who would've thought a 14-year-old could inspire so deeply? Your resilience, strength, and relentless drive continue to move me every single day. Watching you complete your undergraduate studies abroad is a testament to your courage and faith. Thank you for being unapologetically yourself. Your mindset and heart will undoubtedly impact the world.

Many of the people who shaped this journey are mentioned throughout the book, but I want to highlight a few whose roles were foundational. Kim Rodriguez, thank you for asking the hard questions early on—you lit the spark that got this all started. You helped me believe in the power of my story, and in sharing it without reservation.

To Holly Payne, my writing coach—our paths crossed by chance, but I know our connection will outlast this lifetime. "Thank you" feels insufficient. I'm confident our journey together is far from over, and frankly, you might be stuck with me.

To my parents, Art and Judy—your love for our family is immense. You showed Adam and me what a devoted, nurturing family looks like, and that gift has shaped every part of who I am.

To Adam—we will never be able to repay you for what you did for us that night. Thank you, from the deepest part of my soul.

To Alaina's friends and suitemates—meeting you after the shooting could have been painfully awkward, and at first, it was. But it became clear very quickly: you all truly loved one another. You shared a bond built on real friendship. Lauren, you knew her well—multitasking through a Friends marathon while reading and texting all at once. Ashley Mowreader, your edits—especially catching every double space (yes, I left one in here just for you)—meant more than you know. Alicia, I can't begin to understand what it means to survive something so horrific, but I find comfort knowing Alaina was with you that night.

To the Filipino side of our family—your constant, unconditional love has sustained us. Every step, every hug, every silent presence has been deeply felt and appreciated.

To the Pepperdine *Sigma Chi* brothers—whether alumni or active members, your love and solidarity meant so much to us. Just being there when we arrived at Pepperdine meant so much, especially the hike to the Cross and the tribute to rebuild, meant so much. It's funny how little things have changed in the chapter since we founded it over thirty years ago—a comfort in its own way.

Dr. Andy Benton, thank you for your grace and steady leadership of the Pepperdine community during a time of unspeakable tragedy. Your continued support, along with that of Dr. Connie Horton and her incredible team, helped guide us through the fog. Connie, your warmth and compassion were a guiding light.

Tom Joyce—your cover design took my breath away the first time I saw it. The photo you selected has always been one of our favorites.

Jeneen Neeners—Alaina's spiritual Godmother thank you for still coming annually to Thanksgiving even though she was supposed to come with you that November. Your friendship is priceless.

And to Sarah Lane—your gift for photography captured Alaina in all her beauty, warmth, and kindness. The images you created allow others to see what Hannah and I have always known and cherished.

To my early readers—there are too many of you to name here, but please know: your thoughtful feedback gave me the confidence to believe this book could truly make a difference.

To everyone named in these pages—your presence in our journey has made the unbearable a little more bearable. Through your love, and through His love—and through the enduring love we still feel from Alaina—I have found a way forward in helping others with their grief journey.

About the Authors

ARIK HOUSLEY is an author, entrepreneur and public speaker. He has served the Napa Valley community for more than 30 years, operating grocery stores, a winery and an Italian restaurant. An ardent soccer fan and former coach, Housley owns the men's and women's Napa Valley 1839 FC soccer teams. He and his family founded Alaina's Voice Foundation, in honor of their late daughter, to support education, music and mental health initiatives in Napa Valley. As a national speaker, Housley inspires others to "be the positive change" and cultivate compassion and strength in the face of adversity. You can find him on IG @arikjih8, on Substack @arikhousley, and at www.arikhousley.com.

HOLLY LYNN PAYNE is an award-winning, internationally published author, private writing coach, and the host and producer of the Page One Podcast. Her recent bestseller, *Rose Girl*, won a Kirkus starred review and was named Editor's Choice from the Historical Novel Society.
She earned a master's degree from USC, a BA in journalism from the University of Richmond, and has served on the faculty of the California College of the Arts, Academy of Art University, San Francisco State University and Stanford University. Find her on IG @hollylynnpayne and Power of Page One Substack.

A Request to Share the Love

IF *ALWAYS NOVEMBER* moved you, comforted you, or gave you strength, would you consider sharing its message?

This book was born from a father's deepest heartbreak—and my choice to meet unimaginable loss with unshakable love. Your review supports my mission to bring comfort, connection, and healing to others navigating loss.

Here's how you can help spread the word:

- **Post a review** on Amazon. If *Always November* helped you rethink grief—please consider letting others know too.
- **Gift a copy** to a friend, family member, or colleague who may need comfort or courage.
- **Share on social media**—whether it's a quote, your favorite passage, or a photo with the book. Tag me @arik_housley so I can thank you personally.
- **Invite me to speak** at your book club, event, organization, or school. I'm always honored to share the story and the lessons I've learned.

Every share, post, and recommendation helps keep Alaina's light—and legacy of kindness alive. If you're interested in learning more about our foundation, please visit *Alainasvoice.org*.

With heartfelt gratitude,

Arik

Email: *arik@arikhousley.com*
Instagram: *arik_housley*
Book Clubs, Media & Speaking: arikhousley.com

Subscribe to Arik Housley on Substack

www.ingramcontent.com/pod-product-compliance
Lightning Source LLC
Chambersburg PA
CBHW031314160426
43196CB00007B/527